T0063964

PSALM 83:

A New Discovery

PSALM 83:
A New Discovery

ALEXANDER ZEPHYR

PSALM 83: A NEW DISCOVERY

Copyright © 2014 Alexander Zephyr.

Author/Designer of the Front Page Image: Liz Jarnicki

All rights reserved. No part of this book may be used or reproduced by any means, graphic, electronic, or mechanical, including photocopying, recording, taping or by any information storage retrieval system without the written permission of the publisher except in the case of brief quotations embodied in critical articles and reviews.

iUniverse books may be ordered through booksellers or by contacting:

iUniverse
1663 Liberty Drive
Bloomington, IN 47403
www.iuniverse.com
1-800-Authors (1-800-288-4677)

Because of the dynamic nature of the Internet, any web addresses or links contained in this book may have changed since publication and may no longer be valid. The views expressed in this work are solely those of the author and do not necessarily reflect the views of the publisher, and the publisher hereby disclaims any responsibility for them.

Any people depicted in stock imagery provided by Thinkstock are models, and such images are being used for illustrative purposes only.
Certain stock imagery © Thinkstock.

ISBN: 978-1-4917-5074-2 (sc)
ISBN: 978-1-4917-5075-9 (e)

Library of Congress Control Number: 2014918565

Printed in the United States of America.

iUniverse rev. date: 11/12/2014

TABLE OF CONTENTS

INTRODUCTION

Some parts of the Bible befuddle even the most dedicated readers of the world's most sacred text and popular book. The quest to identify the nations of Psalm 83 has incited immense confusion among scholars. There are plenty views and ideas as to which country will take part in this conspiracy to eradicate Israel and which will not; is Psalm 83 a prophecy for the future, an event of the distant past, or it is merely a simple lament and imprecatory prayer of the prophet asking God to help to His people in the fight against their enemies? The Prophet Asaph enumerated the nations that were well known to the ancient world in his time—without tying people's dwellings to certain geographical boundaries. His main goal was to rightly identify these people in the End Time, regardless of their ancient geographical locations. As a seer, he foresaw that the people whom he prophesied about would not remain in the places that they occupied at the time, and would move all over the Earth. Such vision is a gift of prophecy. It is not the geographical places that were important for Asaph, but certain nations that had perpetually hated Israel and would plot against it in the future. His prophecy has never been fulfilled, which is why scholars have treated his writing as predicting the End Time.

Over the course of many long centuries the names of the nations and their locations have changed significantly. It is therefore important to correctly trace and identify the nations of the Asaph prophesy in order to understand it. Knowledge of secular and Biblical history, the writings of the prophets, and the opinions of the sages of the Talmud, together with an understanding of contemporary geopolitical events, is key to deciphering the enigmatic puzzles of Psalm 83. To understand the future course of world history in the highly complex field of international relations, one has to be able to correctly identify the old nations of the prophecy qua their modern-day equivalents. Keeping this task in mind, let us begin to unravel the controversies of Psalm 83.

"They have said, Come, and let us cut them off from being a nation; that the name of Israel may be no more in remembrance. For they have consulted together with one consent: they are confederate against you: the tabernacles of Edom, and the Ishmaelites; of Moab, and the Hagarenes; Gebal, and Ammon, and Amalek; the Philistines with the inhabitants of Tyre; Assur also is joined with them. They have helped the children of Lot. Selah" (Psalms 83:4-8).

All the Arab and Muslim countries surrounding Israel are well represented in this murderous coalition. We may easily attest to the fact that this prophecy aims to reveal the future by the fact that such an alliance of ten participants in a plot against Israel has yet to happen. One cannot find this particular group of nations conspiring against Israel anywhere in Scripture. The state of Israel has not been in existence since the Assyrian conquest of 722 BCE to 1948 ACE. As Lang's Commentary notes, "The ten nations, who are here enumerated as being combined against Israel, are never mentioned elsewhere as enemies allied at the same time and for the purpose of annihilating Israel." The Anchor Bible makes the same assertion: "History transmits no record of the national crisis when the nations enumerated in this Psalm formed a league to wipe out Israel." Only one passage of verse 8 – "Assur also is joined with them: they have helped the children of Lot" – clearly indicates that Psalm 83 is not simply a lament or an imprecatory prayer of the 10th century BCE, but a full-scale prophecy for our age with concrete participants and solid details of their actions. Later on, in a proper place, we will explain why Assur comes to help Ammon and Moab (the children of Lot), the nature of its help, and what modern Jordan will require.

There are clear indications that this prophecy aims for the End Times. This is commonly accepted view. And because Psalm 83 aims to reveal the future, we can clearly recognize today (on first sight) the countries of the confederacy that will attack Israel in order to "cut [it] off from being a nation": the Palestinians of the West Bank (Edom), Saudi Arabia (the Ishmaelites), Hamas, the Palestinians of Gaza (Philistines, Amalekites), Lebanon and Hezbollah (Gebal and Tyre),

Jordan (Ammon and Moab), Egypt (the Hagarenes), Syria and Iraq (former Assyria)—ten nations all together. Supposedly, these countries will take part in this bloody crusade. The very first in order is Edom. He has never forgotten nor forgiven Jacob, who "took away [his] birthright and stole [his] blessing" (Genesis 27:36) in ancient time. An age-old hatred of his brother Jacob, a thirst for revenge and an irreconcilable wish to kill his brother—all of these will move Edom to play an important role in the confrontation with Israel and fulfill the prophecies of the End Times.

Bill Salus and others theologians think that Edom represents the Palestinians and their "tents of refugees." Salus praises the Prophet Asaph's ability to foresee the Palestinian refugees today as the tents of Edom. Thus, the present Palestinian refugee crisis serves as the rallying call of the Psalm 83 confederacy. He even applies the Biblical definition of people living in tents as refugees or occupiers of the military encampments of attacking armies. And because the Palestinians with their refugee camps are first in the list of nations plotting against Israel in Psalm 83, he treats them as "the stars of the prophetic show." In this book, we will see how mistaken this author is in identifying Edom with the Palestinians and their "camps of refugees." He also includes Syria and Iraq in this confederation as substitutes for Assur, despite the fact that those nations are not mentioned in Asaph's prophecy. The ancient Assyrian people are not synonymous with the Aramaean people of Syria – although they are Semites by race – because they belong to two different ancestries. In addition, he identifies the Hagarenes with Egypt on the premise that Hagar was the "Egyptian's matriarch." Meanwhile, Egypt, as Syria and Iraq, is not mentioned in the list of plotters in Psalm 83. Later on we will dispute these identifications, and at the same time attempt to ascertain the true descendants of Edom, Egypt, Assur and others.

Herbert W. Armstrong believed that Edom was not identified with the Palestinians or their "tents of refugees," but with the Republic of Turkey; the Hagarenes anciently dwelt in the land now known as Syria, and countries such as Iran, Iraq, and Egypt are absent from this confederation because, as he suggested, they were already defeated in the preceding war by the king of the north (Daniel 11:40-43). In his opinion, Assur is modern Germany. This version deserves careful attention and ought to be considered the most probable and truthful. We will elaborate on this theory in more detail later in the book.

Other scholars have interpreted Edom as Rome (Italy), Germany, Spain, Mexico, Turkey, and so on. The Hagarenes are identified with Iraqis or Syrians, the Philistines with Amalek. Attempts to identify the nations of Psalm 83:6-8 have caused a great deal of confusion among scholars. The names of countries such as Germany and Turkey are not found in Scripture, which is not particularly unusual—the Bible does not mention many nations by their modern names. In ancient times the names of these nations were different. It was according to God's divine purpose that these names were included in Scripture, so that we might trace them in order to learn who these nations are today and what place and role they play in global politics.

THE THEOLOGY OF
STEVEN M. COLLINS

There are some theologians who think that Psalm 83 is not a prophecy of the future at all, but an account of events which took place in the past. Among them is the prominent Bible scholar Steve Collins, who insists that Psalm 83 is not prophetic and has no application to the future because its language does not contain words like "time of the end," "in that day," "latter days" and other phrases that suggest its relevance to our age. In addition, Collins has arrived at the conclusion that Psalm 83 is nothing more than a description of the Great War that King David conducted against the Mesopotamian nations led by "Assur," that is, the Assyrian Empire. This war was provoked by the Ammonites and Moabites who are "the children of Lot," and Assur, with the rest of the vassal kings, came to help the children of Lot. "There can be little doubt that 1Chronicles 19 and Psalm 83 refer to the same war in circa 990 BCE," Collins argues in his Prophecy Updates and Commentary Blog.

From our point of view, this author's conclusion is incorrect and not supported by Scriptural evidence. There is an immense difference between the wars conducted by King David in 1Chronicles 19 or 2Chronicles 10 and the coming war of Psalm 83. There is no doubt that the wars in David's time happened and we know the final result of them, as the Bible and history have revealed. The Israelites defeated Ammonites, Syrians and other allies from Mesopotamia. Meanwhile, the war of Psalm 83 is of the future, and the fate of the bloodthirsty genocidal coalition of the Asaph prophecy will also be decided in the latter days. The names of the nations and their numbers are considerably different too. If in the time of David the first wars against Israel were fought by Ammonites, Syrians and allies from Mesopotamia (probably Assyrians and Babylonians)—all together three or four known nations—in the future wars described by Prophet Asaph, the confederacy consists of ten nations. Many nations, such as Edom, Gebal, Amalek, and Ishmael, were not even mentioned in the previous wars. The children of Lot were not completed because Moab, the brother of Ammon, who had been defeated by the Israelites earlier, did not participate. Even the reasons for these wars are not the same. The Ammonites provoked David to war by humiliating his ambassadors of good will by "shaving off their beards and cutting off their garments in the middle hard by their buttocks, and sent them away" (1 Chronicles19:4). The Ammonites acted this way not because they were strong and brave to fight the Israelites by themselves. They were pushed by Syria and Assyria, their allies, who wanted to challenge Israel for supremacy in the region. In future wars, the children of Lot (basically Moab and Ammon of Jordan) will continue their provocative tactics to unleash war against Israel, knowing that they will be protected by their powerful friends (that is, Assur, Edom and other members of the coalition). And, of course, there was no manifestly expressed reason "to cut them off, that the name of Israel may be no more in remembrance" in the David wars, as the plotters swore in Psalm 83.

Another important difference between these wars is that in the time of David, Israel was represented by the powerful United Kingdom of the Twelve Tribes; in the time of Psalm 83's future wars, the Israelis will be represented by the three tribes of Judah, Benjamin, and most of Levy, known as the modern-day Jewish people. It is only during this war or after its end that the Messiah ben Joseph will arrive and reunite all the Twelve Tribes of the whole House of Israel that they together will be able to bring "the fist of God's judgment" on attacking enemies and may later face the invasion and death of the hordes of Gog and Magog on the Mountains of Israel during the ultimate war in human history. Also, Collins believes that Gog's attack will not take place on the very territory of the Biblical land of Israel, but in the countries of Europe, North America, Australia, New Zealand, and South Africa—the geographical places where the people of Israeli origin (the Ten Tribes) are located.

This conclusion is not Scriptural. God clearly states that He will bring Gog "against My Land" (Ezekiel 38:16). "My

Land" does not mean any other lands where the Ten Tribes of Israel dwell in exile; it surely means the Holy Land, the home of the whole House of Israel. There is another hint in Ezekiel 38:12 that Gog will attack the people "that dwell in the midst of the land." All of the translators of Scripture have understood that "the midst of the land" is the Land of Israel. There is strong evidence in Ezekiel that the war campaign of Gog and his tragic finale will take place on the mountains of Israel. One more example will illustrate this: "Thou shalt fall upon the mountains of Israel. I will give unto Gog a place there for graves in Israel, the valley of the passengers on the east of the sea" (Ezekiel 39:4, 11). In rabbinical tradition, the geographical places mentioned in Ezekiel were well known to the Jewish people. Targum identifies the sea of Verse 11 as the Sea of Ginossar, that is, the Sea of Galilee (Radak). Ginossar was known as the Royal Gardens for its luscious produce and attracted many tourists, "passengers" and "travelers" (Bereishis Rabbah 98). The prophet, in connection with Gog's defeat and burial, speaks of one 'field,' one 'valley,' one 'city,' one 'Sea,' one 'Land of Israel'. Is it not obvious that Ezekiel 38 and 39 portray the Holy Land as the target of Gog's attack against Israel?

Although this author is incorrect regarding this particular assumption, the theme of the Lost Ten Tribes of Israel in exile is very familiar to him, and could be instructive for Bill Salus and Joel Richardson, who in their writings make no distinction between Judah and Israel, but in all instances call the Israelites "Jews." Regarding the exodus from Egypt, they speak of Jews; so too of the handing down of the Torah on Mount Zion, of Joshua's defeat of Canaan and of the war of Gog and Magog. Thus Salus, analyzing the prophecy of Isaiah 11:11, contends that God will regather the Jews into Israel from the nations a second time. In his mind, this is the one of the prerogatives required for the fulfillment of Psalm 83. However, an attentive reading of verses 11 and 12 shows that the Prophet Isaiah spoke not only of the Jews (who had already returned to the Promised Land and established the state of Israel in 1948), but also of the lost Ten Tribes of Israel: "And he shall set up an ensign for the nations, and shall assemble the outcasts of Israel, and gather together the dispersed of Judah from the four corners of the earth" (Isaiah 11:12). The meaning is, "He shall gather together the outcasts and dispersed of both Israel and Judah, both male and female." In the first Babylonian restoration Judah alone was restored; in the future – second – restoration both are expressly mentioned in accordance with the prophecies of Ezekiel (37: 16-19) and Jeremiah (3:18). Undoubtedly the second restoration of Judah and Israel will be in the perfect spiritual belief in the Almighty God of Israel.

THE THEORIES OF
JOEL RICHARDSON
AND BILL SALUS

Another well-published and well-known theologian, Joel Richardson, also doubts the prophetic significance of Psalm 83, saying that its contents are not consistent with Scripture. In a published entitled article "Which nations does Psalm 83 really include?", Richardson contends that the writer, Asaph, is not as valid as the prophets of the Bible and that his writings look more like an imprecatory prayer of the 10th century BCE. Richardson is more inclined to call Psalm 83 a national prayer or lament: "Such a Psalm would not be considered a prophecy in the sense of that which was uttered by the biblical prophets." He doubts that Psalm 83 predicts the imminent war in the Middle East and that Israel is about to defeat its surrounding neighbors and expand its territory to the Biblical geographical borders, as God promised. In order to avoid angering the majority of his Christian colleagues who have accepted Asaph's Psalm 83 as an important prophecy aimed at our age, Richardson mollifies his position and admits that "Psalm 83 is a prophetic Psalm beyond its original context as an imprecatory prayer." This attitude of compromise results in slippery arguments and a conclusion that lacks solid and concrete answers on the subject—all distinctive features of Richardson's theology. Speaking of Asaph as the author of Psalm 83, the Bible testifies that he was a seer—a prophet— and the psalm is a prophecy no different than any other prophecy in the Bible. Not only was Asaph a musician, singer, and poet, he was also a full-scale Biblical prophet, and so were his sons who prophesied with lyres, with harps, and with cymbals (2 Chronicles 29:30; 1 Chronicles 25:1). Richardson is not sure that, "in fact, Psalm 83 represents a specific future war." He cannot with certainty name the participants of this war, arguing with Salus about the inclusion or exclusion of Assyria, Iraq, Syria, and Turkey, and avoiding straight answers. At least Salus names countries according to his understanding without wandering away from the subject, albeit wrongly. Both Salus and Richardson are invested in the idea that the inclusion of this or that country on the list of plotters depends on the territory that ancient Assyria possessed in the past. If it covered the territories of Syria, Iraq, and Turkey—then these countries must be included in the confederation under the name of Assur. Richardson criticizes Salus for including Syria but not Turkey. In other words, Richardson substitutes Assur with Turkey, Syria, and Iraq. And what is the reason given for such a decision? Because the Assyrian Empire at the time of Asaph fully or partially occupied the territories of these countries, so over 3,000 thousand years later the name of Assur automatically belongs to them. As he puts it in his words, "Analysts of Psalm 83 have included both Iraq and Syria in their coming invasion scenario, but never Turkey. Yet the reality is that the Assyrian Kingdom during the time the Psalm was written included quite a bit more of modern Turkey than Syria. This is significant, of course, because Turkey features so prominently in the Ezekiel 38 & 39 prophecy."

Richardson has many followers who blindly praise his prophetic expertise in connection with Assyria and the countries of its substitution. One of those followers, Terry Malone, states that the Assur of Psalm 83 could comprise many modern nations besides Iraq and Syria, such as Turkey, Iran, Kuwait, Azerbaijan, Armenia, and Georgia—all of this is on premise that the Assyrian Empire in ancient times "included substantial portions" of these countries' territories—and that we should therefore substitute Assur with these nations.

This is what Richardson calls "the geographic-correlation theory" of identifying the ancient nations in order to correlate them with the requirements of future prophecies. According to this theory, it does not matter whether the original nation migrated out of the region a long time ago and became different country, bearing a different name, dwelling in a different part of the world, or even if it disappeared from the face of the earth; nor does it matter that the same region has been occupied by a different race or nation, which has nothing to do with original inhabitants (Assyrians). The absurdity of this theory renders it unworthy of comment.

One of his opponents, Sean Osborne, argued that in the hundred year period circa 1000 to 900 BCE – when Asaph wrote Psalm 83 –Assur (Assyria) was in full retreat from the lands it had occupied to the west of the Euphrates River, and was centered in modern-day Iraq in the Tigris and Euphrates valleys. The territories of Syria and Turkey at the time of the Prophet Asaph were not occupied by Assyria. To prove the point, Osborne submitted a map courtesy of the Assyrian National News Agency and rhetorically asked: "Who knows Assyrian history better, the modern descendants of ancient Assyria or Joel Richardson? Sorry, but one cannot cook a 'Turkey' that is not in the Psalm 83 pot."

Richardson's uncertainty in determining the countries of the secret confederacy against Israel is so obvious that it is hard to hide. Thus, he writes, "Among the names that are clearly not mentioned in the Psalm 83 coalition is Aram, the capital of which was Damascus." So, may we ask, if Syria is not mentioned in this prophecy, why does Richardson agree with Salus and revise the prophecy to feed his preconceived ideas, even expanding Syria to include Iraq and Turkey, countries that are not mentioned in Psalm 83? Note: Turkey, in fact, is mentioned in this prophecy, very much so, but not as a substitute for Assur. We will examine the matter later, when we discuss the identity of Edom. On the subject of Egypt's participation in the confederacy, Richardson rightly disagrees with Salus, saying that the Hagrites are not Egyptians, but he does not say positively what nation they represent today. His conclusion that "if the Psalmist had intended Egypt to be included among his list of nations, he would simply have listed Egypt" may be directed against him: Syria and Iraq are not listed either—why does he apply these names in Psalm 83?

There is another method of identifying the ancient nations of Psalm 83 from the perspective of modern realities—by tracing their bloodline ancestry and migrations down through history. Richardson does not like this method and harshly criticizes those "untrained Bible teachers" who use this method of interpretation. He insists that the geographic-correlation method of identifying the Old Testament nations is the best because it is universally utilized by the scholars and commentators of the Bible: "For the simple sake of truth and love for the Scriptures," he says, "it was important to demonstrate some of the ways in which the popular view of Psalm 83 is simply not in accordance with the Scriptures." Did he really demonstrate the Biblical truth in interpreting Psalm 83? Let our readers answer this question.

We have already shown through the examples of Edom and Assur how uncertain and incorrect this method is. To understand the future course of world history in the highly complex field of international relations, one has to be able to correctly identify the old nations of the prophecy. It can be done by analyzing Scripture, historical records of particular nations, and their bloodline origins, national character traits that remain consistent over the centuries, migrations, art, archeology, language, religion, etc. All of these things may provide important clues in properly interpreting the prophecy.

Salus also loves the theory of "the geographic-correlation" and uses it similarly to Richardson, especially in his quest to resolve the puzzling question of the absence of Iran from the list of conspirators in Psalm 83. "The pitfall of connecting modern-day Iran with Assyria is that during the psalmist's time, Assyria only comprised much of what is today northern Syria and part of Iraq," he says. If Assyria comprised the territory of Iran (Persia) during the time of the Prophet Asaph, then the name of Assur necessarily includes Iran; if not, then this is the reason why Iran is absent from the list of plotters. The matter is categorically short, simple and clear. The participation of Iraq and Syria does not cause any problems for him, because he supposedly knows from history that ancient Assyria during the psalmist's time comprised much of the territory of modern Syria and part of Iraq. For him it is more than enough to include these countries in the list of plotters, regardless of the fact that Syria and Iraq are not home to Assyrians and represent distinct races and peoples. In doing so, Salus rejects the possibility of Assyria existing today and ignores the numerous Biblical prophecies about Assur in the End Times. Iran was never part of the Assyrian Empire, so he cannot connect it to Assyria.

But what is the real reason that Iran is not listed in Psalm 83? In his analysis Salus tries to make the case that although

Iran is the enemy of Israel, its population is not Arabic but primarily Persian in descent, and Arabs and Persians have a long-standing history of warring against each other dating as far back as the Persian conquest of the Babylonians around 539 BCE. In modern history, Iraq and Iran fought against each other from 1980 until 1988. Presently, many Arab countries are deeply concerned about Iran's nuclear ambitions; the traditional animosity between Arabs and Persians, and the fact that Sunni Muslims of Arab descent are participating in the confederacy, could explain Iran's absence from Psalm 83. Iran is Persian and the confederation of Psalm 83 is dominated by the Arab population; this could be the reason why Iran is not a participatory alongside its Arab proxies.

Salus does not stop here. He somehow feels that the explanations given are not enough, so he offers another possibility on the subject of Iran: "The Arab versus Persian argument is not the only possible reason Iran refrains from participating in the Psalm 83 war. Possibility number two is that part of Iran may be temporarily incapacitated at the time, according to a generally overlooked prophecy issued by Jeremiah." In fact, this idea is a central argument of his new book *Nuclear Showdown in Iran, Revealing the Ancient Prophecy of Elam*. Of all the possibilities he suggests, this one is the most verisimilar; it is in line with our understanding of the prophecies concerned, and deserves close attention. Iran may be temporarily incapacitated at the time, according to the Prophet Jeremiah's account (49:35-36): "Thus says the

LORD of hosts; Behold, I will break the bow of Elam, the chief of their might. And upon Elam will I bring the four winds from the four quarters of heaven, and will scatter them toward all those winds; and there shall be no nation where the outcasts of Elam shall not come."

Wait a minute, our reader may say. Up to this point Salus has been discussing the nation of Iran; how is it that he now refers to a prophecy which concerns the nation of Elam? What do these two nations have in common? Good question. The nation of Iran was not known to the world under the name of "Iran." Throughout most of its history this nation was called "Persia." Beginning in 1935, the ruler of Persia, Reza Shah Pahlavi, issued a decree asking the international community to call his country "Iran." Nowadays both terms are common and used interchangeably; "Persia" is used mostly in a historical and cultural sense, "Iran" mostly in a political sense. It was the Medes who unified Persia as a nation and empire in 625 BCE. In the time of the Persian King Darius (522-486 BCE), the Elamites were defeated, lost their independence, were fully absorbed into the Persian Empire, and became the Persian-Iranian people, the same way as the Hittites were absorbed by the Assyrian Empire before and became the Assyrians. The millennia of Elamite-Persian interactions and the Arabian conquest of Persia in 633-656 ACE, have united these two nations into one unified Islamic nation called Persia. This historic transformation was confirmed by Flavius in his *Antiquities of the Jews*, chapter

VI, paragraph 4:"For Elam left behind him the Elamites, the ancestors of the Persians." It is important to note that Persia is identified with Japheth's son Teras (Genesis 10:2). In connecting this information with the prophecy of Jeremiah 49:35-36, it should be added that an ancient Elam is situated in the territory of Iran by the very northern end of the Persian Gulf and down along with the west cost of Iran on the edge of the southwestern part of the Iranian plateau, which is modern Khuzestan. But what is most important and relevant is the fact that the historical Elam resides on the territory of the Iranian Bushehr Province, the home of nuclear facilities and an acting nuclear reactor. It is amazing that 2600 years ago, the Prophet Jeremiah accurately predicted Elam-Iran's possession of the nuclear weapon (referred to as a bow), which is the "chief source of their might." The judgment against Elam is very specific and the language used cannot be found anywhere else in Scripture. The nuclear ambitions of Iran are well known and have garnered the attention of the world. Now, the question is: by whose hands will God cause this ancient prophecy to be fulfilled? There are some rumors and expectations that Iran will use the Bushehr nuclear plant as a base to build nuclear weapons to destroy Israel and threaten other nations on its way to establishing the Islamic Caliphate and achieving world domination. Since Israel has declared on a few occasions that it will do everything possible not to allow Iran to become a nuclear power, Salus thinks that it will be Israel who attack and destroy the Bushehr nuclear plant. That is what he writes in his article "Are Jeremiah 49 and Ezekiel 38 the Same Prophetic Events?": "Israel, the Arab Gulf states and the international community are extremely concerned about Iran's nuclear pursuits, and someday soon Israel may be compelled to attack Iran. Such an attack could be what triggers the fulfillment of this world changing prophecy."

Salus' opinion is strongly supported by the theologian John McTernan, the founder of Defend and Proclaim the Faith Ministries, who in his article "Elam/Iran in the Latter-Days" says that Israel's attack on the Bushehr nuclear reactor could cause a nuclear holocaust and humanitarian crisis of unseen proportions. A disaster of epic biblical proportion will finally arrive in the Middle East. The past nuclear disasters of Chernobyl and Fukushima would not even be comparable. It is also possible that World War III could commence as a result of this attack. Both authors take the words of the prophet "there shall be no nation where the outcasts of Elam shall not come" to mean that the Arabian Gulf will become a cesspool of radioactive contamination and whomever is saved will be scattered into the nations of the world. That is what the prophecy says. God's judgment of Elam has not occurred in recorded history but will be fulfilled in the future. McTernan adds that Elam was a fierce enemy of Israel. It participated in two attacks against Jerusalem, first with the Assyrians and later on with the Babylonians. Now Israel is once again a nation and ancient Elam/Iran is again trying to destroy Israel and capture Jerusalem. Furthermore, commenting on

Jeremiah 49:38, McTernan states that God will break not only Elam but also its militant religion of Islam, which seeks to destroy Israel and take over the world. Instead of Islam, it will be the God of Israel who will establish His rule and authority over the entire world, including the people of Iran, as it says, "I will set My throne in Elam" (verse 38).

Salus correctly notes that the prophetic events described in Jeremiah 49 and Ezekiel 38 are distinct in subject matter, geography, and time. Also, to his credit, he accurately observes that Iran will experience particular double trouble in the end time. The battle fields will be different too: the judgment on Elam will take place on the territory of the Central Western region of modern Iran; the downfall of Persia and the rest of the Gog-Magog hordes will happen in the land of Israel.

However, a few questions remain unanswered. If Elam-Iran was defeated and scattered all over the world in Jeremiah 49, then why is Iran again represented, under the name of Persia, as an ally of Gog's armies in Ezekiel 38 and 39? The answer is not complicated and can be found in these words of the prophet: "But it shall come to pass in the latter days that I will bring again the captivity of Elam, says the Lord." This verse conveys two meanings. First, the events described in Jeremiah 49 concerning the judgment on Elam will happen much earlier and precede the Gog and Magog war (and the events of Psalm 83 as well). Second, the events of Ezekiel 38 and 39 will occur in the distant future, as indicated in the prophecy; "in the latter days" God will return the Persians to their own land. It would take a long period of time for the Persian people to recover from nuclear disaster, to regain independence, and to acquire the economic and military strength to join the forces of Gog in the final attack against Israel. It seems that the powerful lessons of the past will not prevail over the perpetual hatred of Israel and its God. By its own design, Iran will meet the God of judgment and find its graves on the mountains of Israel, as the prophecy clearly attests (Ezekiel 39:4).

And by whose hands will the Almighty enact His judgment on Elam? "The only way to prevent Iran from becoming a nuclear power is for Israel to attack Iran's nuclear installations," says Caroline B. Glick, the senior Middle East Fellow at the center for Security Policy in Washington. Although there is plenty of evidence, based on history and modern geopolitics, that it will be Israel that will attack the nuclear facilities of Iran in order to secure and protect its own survival, we do not fully support this thesis. Three years ago, in our book *The State of Israel: Its Friends and Enemies*, we wrote: "The United Europe under the undisputed leadership of Germany will attack Iran and its allies in a blitzkrieg manner and take over all the Middle East and North Africa, defeating the king of the south (Iran) and conquering all its allies—Iraq, Syria, Egypt, Libya, and Ethiopia" (Daniel 11:43). The prophecy of Daniel (11:40-45) is of immense importance here, serving as a necessary link in the chain of future prophesied events under discussion. Analyzing these prophecies, we can understand that the wars of the king of the north (Assur-Germany) and the king of the south (the short-lived Iranian Islamic coalition) will take place prior to the events of Psalm 83. As the reader can see, all kind of explanations have been given on the subject of Iran's absence from Psalm 83, save the one which clearly and simply tells us that Iran is the king of the south of Daniel 11:36-45, and its absence from the confederacy of plotters is explained by the fact that Iran was defeated and subjugated immediately before the war of Psalm 83 by the king of the north, which is a German-led European Union. If these authors paid proper attention to the prophecies of Daniel in connection with Psalm 83 and Ezekiel 38 and 39, they would not make so many basic mistakes in identifying the nations; there would not be disputations and misunderstandings about the participant-nations of these wars, the sequence of events, timing, and other important issues; and modern-day Turkey (Edom) and Assur (Germany) would not be dismissed as possibilities. It would also be known to them that this confederation of nations "consists not only of Arab states and terrorist populations, which presently share common borders with Israel," but also of Edomites-Turks, Assur-Germans and other nations (the EU) as well. And they do not have to share common borders with Israel nor must they be all Muslims, as theologian Dr. Chuck Missler claims after Salus, because Assur and the ten kings of the European Empire are located in Europe and represent the Vatican, which is the heart and soul of Christian Catholicism. We will elaborate on all of this in more detail in Chapter XII.

Bill Salus is certain that Psalm 83 aims to predict the future, and his analysis, rightly or wrongly, is fixed on its future fulfillment. For Richardson, Psalm 83 is an ancient imprecatory prayer without prophetic significance. Richardson's position is shared by Dr. Thomas Ice who also thinks that Psalm 83 is a national lament which includes prayer and imprecations. Since there is no recorded response by God to Prophet Asaph's request, then the Lord did not provide a prophecy in Psalm 83. Therefore, he says, it would be impossible for Salus' version of the fulfillment of Psalm 83 to occur before the prophecy of Ezekiel 38 and 39. The Biblical text of Psalm 83 does not contain a prophecy no matter what some contend when they refer to the Psalm 83 war. "I challenge anyone to show me a prophetic portion or statement in Psalm 83! There will be no Psalm 83 war. In my opinion, those who are willing to base their end-time views on mere speculation and inference will suffer the same fate as others who have played this game for the last 2,000 years—disrespect and disdain," concludes Dr. Ice.

Richardson, nevertheless, allows the possibility that "if it is a prophecy, the view that it is referring to a specific war that takes place prior to and distinct from other antichristic end time battles stands in direct conflict with Scripture." What does he mean? In his opinion, the prophecy of Psalm 83 is impossible because Israel could not possibly defeat Edom and

Moab before the appearance of the Messiah. In his words, "The Psalm 83 theory wrongly interprets the prophets, and the most worrisome error of this is that it takes the righteous judgments of Jesus and relocates them to mere men." Astonishing nonsense! How many prophecies of wars and God's judgments have been fulfilled in the past? How many times has Israel won or lost battles according to God's will? The God Almighty is in full control of earth, and it is He who decides whether to perform His work by the hands of His people Israel or any other servants, or by Himself.

Richardson states that the nations of Psalm 83 will not be destroyed in a war *several years before* the return of the Messiah. But who says that such scenario would unfold? Quite the opposite: it is the Messiah who will carry out judgments and utterly annihilate the nations of God's wrath. Again, it is God's decision how to carry out His Judgments: "You are My war club, My weapon for battle— with you I shatter nations, with you I destroy kingdoms" (Jeremiah 51:20). What could possibly be clearer proof of the point than these words of the Almighty? He has his purposes in choosing such a course of action. There are times and places when God executes judgments by Himself, as it is recorded in the Bible: "And it came to pass that night, that the angel of the LORD went out, and struck in the camp of the Assyrians a hundred and eighty-five thousand: and when they arose early in the morning, behold, these were all dead bodies" (2 Kings 19:35; Isaiah 37:36). Concerning the Gog and Magog judgment, God declared that it is He personally who will deal with them: "I will bring you upon the mountains of Israel, and then I will strike your bow from your left hand and make your arrows drop from your right hand. You will fall on the open field; for it is I who have spoken, declares the Lord GOD" (Ezekiel 39:2-5). The same declaration is found in the Midrash: "I have many messengers whom I can send into battle. But the war against Gog and Magog I shall wage Myself. Their destruction shall be complete" (Esther Rabbah 7:23). Another example is the king of the north, representing the European Union under the leadership of Assur-Germany. There is a prophecy in Isaiah predicting that this king of the north – the Prophet calls him "the King of Assyria" – will, after defeating the king of the south (Iran) and its allies, "enter into the glorious land" (Daniel 11:41) as a counterfeit peacekeeper, and plot with the enemies of Israel to annihilate the Israelites and take over their land and Jerusalem (Psalm 83:3-8, 12). God emphasizes through the Prophet Isaiah that He will personally judge the king of the north, or Assur: "Assyria will fall by no human sword; a sword, not of mortals, will devour them. They will flee before the sword and their young men will be put to forced labor" (Isaiah 31:8). And, indeed, Daniel 11:45 confirms that the king of the north will not be successful in his ungodly plans, and that "he shall come to his end, and none shall help him." These words testify that God will personally and directly intervene to punish Assyria, which is the king of the north, that is, Assur-Germany of Psalm 83:8. It is important to note that these judgments will be enacted by His will. Contrary to Salus' opinion that all ten of the "inner ring" conspirators of Psalm 83 will be defeated by the Israeli Defense Forces (IDF), the Bible says that Assur, the leading power of the confederacy (outer circle), will be judged and defeated by God.

Numbers (24:17-19), which Richardson refers to as evidence, indeed speak of the future Israelite Messiah, anticipated by many Hebrew prophets. The task of the Messiah is much broader than to defeat Moab and Edom. The prophet Obadiah says that Edom will be destroyed by the *House of Jacob* according to the Word of the Lord (Obadiah 1:18). By the way, here is an enlightening revelation that not many scholars of the Bible have realized: "the House of Jacob" means all the Twelve Tribes of Israel, which also means that by the time of this Judgment of Edom, the King Messiah will have already come and united the House of Judah and the House of Joseph according to the two sticks (Ezekiel 37:19-22) and brought them home to the Promised Land. This reunification at the beginning of the Messianic Age will take place under the leadership of the Messiah; this task will be one of his highest priorities.

Here goes the veracity of Richardson's theory that the war of Psalm 83 and the defeat of the enemies by Israelite forces is impossible without the arrival of the Messiah. At the battle of Jerusalem in the latter years, the besieged Israeli forces will destroy attacking Arab and Muslim nations, as the Bible describes: "The House of Judah shall devour all the people round about; on the right hand and on the left hand" (Zechariah 12:6). The same story is told by the Prophet Isaiah. First, Joseph and Judah will reunite, which definitely point out the presence of the Messiah among them, and then "They shall fly upon the shoulders of the Philistines towards the west; they shall spoil them of the east together: they shall lay their hands upon Edom and Moab; and the children of Ammon shall obey them" (Isaiah11:14). And more of the same: "And I will lay My vengeance upon Edom by the hand of MY people Israel: and they shall do in Edom according to Mine anger and according to My fury; and they shall know My vengeance, saith the Lord GOD" (Ezekiel 25:14). "My people Israel" confirms that all the Twelve Tribes of Israel will execute God's judgments on Edom. If the prophet meant only the Jewish people, he would simply have said "Judah" or "the House of Judah." Denying these Words of God is an insult to the prophets and the Holy Scripture.

Richardson criticizes Salus for his statement that as an outcome of the conspiratorial confederacy of Arab-Muslim nations against Israel, the Israelites will retaliate and defeat them and repossess their lands to the Biblical borders, according to the Word of the Almighty. "Of course, for those familiar with the region, the idea of Israel actually occupying Egypt, Jordan, Syria and Saudi Arabia is quite a wild, if not a completely impossible scenario to imagine," he says. But, really, what is wrong with Salus' statement? He repeats, to his credit, precisely what the prophets said. If one takes a look at Genesis 15, Exodus 23, Numbers 34 and Ezekiel 47, one realizes that the Biblical land of Israel is not tiny at all. Expanded to the prophesied borders, the land of Greater Israel from the Nile to the Euphrates will include the eastern part of Egypt, Sinai, Lebanon and Jordan, parts of Saudi Arabia, Syria, Iraq and Turkey. It is estimated that the Promised Land is eight times the size of Texas. Salus rightly notes that as a result of Israel's military victories over aggressive surrounding nations, "Israel's borders are enlarged, prosperity increases, and national stature is enhanced." This is a proper scriptural observation. He would not likely mind if we added that the situation described above would lead directly to Ezekiel 38:8& 11 which speak of the important terms of Gog's invasion of Israel—that is Israel security. "I will go up to the land of unwalled villages; I will go to them that are at rest, that dwell safely, all of them dwelling without walls, and having neither bars nor gates" (Ezekiel 38:11). The emphasis on the words "all of them" supplies additional proof that the House of Jacob was reunited and living in the Land of Israel, which means that the King Messiah had been already revealed. That condition of Israel's peace and safety would be possible only if the Israelites successfully used the "fist of God's judgments" to defeat their enemies and enlarged their territory to the prophesied borders. The war of Psalm 83 will make these goals possible.

For Richardson it is unbelievable that "the idea that Israel, a single nation with approximately 6 million Jews, will subdue and concurrently occupy several nations with a total population of approximately 170 million Arabs." Again, we have to reveal to him a little secret that may destroy his distrust in the words of God's prophets. It is true that the Israelis constitute 6 million people, but it is also true that their brothers and sisters of the Ten Tribes in exile account for approximately another 500 to 600 million people, a force that the world must reckon with! There are plenty of prophecies in the Bible speaking of the reunification of the whole House of Jacob in the End Time, at the advent of the Messiah's coming. Take a look at Isaiah 11, which speaks of the beginning of the messianic age (verses 1-9); then read how Jewish people will reunite with the Israelite people, and how "the adversaries of Judah shall be cut off" (verses 11-13). Who are those adversaries of Judah in the latter days? They are the nations of the Psalm 83! And what will the united Israel of the Twelve Tribes do? Read the answer for yourself: "But they shall fly on the shoulders of the Philistines toward the west; they shall spoil them of the east together: they shall lay their hand on Edom and Moab; and the children of Ammon shall obey them" (verse 14). What does it mean that "they shall fly on shoulders?" It means that Judah and Ephraim, in the words of Gill, "shall not only agree among themselves, but cheerfully join together against the common enemy; shoulder to shoulder, with one consent, to smite the Philistines, Edom,

Moab, and Ammon." And who will lead the Israelites to battle? Their Commander-in-Chief, their King Messiah. It will be the time of the prophesied Messianic Wars. We hope that this is a satisfactory explanation.

Richardson does not believe that this specific prophetic war of Psalm 83 is distinct from the battle of Gog and Magog or any other wars, and he challenges those scholars who think otherwise. He reproaches their theories as "assumptions" and "unscriptural." Although he does not state his position clearly enough, as usual, what we gather is that he thinks the war depicted in Psalm 83 is identical to the war of Gog and Magog described in Ezekiel 38 and 39. "A closer examination of both texts reveals that it is far more likely that these two passages speak of the same war," he says. Based on little, if any, evidence, he uses Turkey as the country mentioned in both wars. But does he understand what nation the modern Islamic Republic of Turkey represents? It does not seem so. He identifies Edom in Psalm 83, as Salus does, with the Palestinians and their camps of refugees or with the people of southern Jordan, the geographical location of the former Edom Kingdom on Mount Seir. Again, he stubbornly sticks to his "territorial theory," ignoring the fact that Edomites no longer live in southern Jordan, and the people who settled there are of different race and descent. His interpretation does not correspond with Scripture. In this book, we devote a separate chapter to Edom in order to fully support the position that it is the modern Republic of Turkey and compatible with neither the Palestinians with their camps of refugees nor the people of southern Jordan.

The fact is that Iran, Egypt, Syria, Iraq, Libya and Ethiopia are not mentioned, and indeed totally excluded, among the nations attacking Israel in Psalm 83 for reasons that will be discuss later. Edom-Turkey with its historical allies of Ammon and Moab (Jordan) is not presented as a participant in the wars between the king of the north and the king of the south in Daniel because it will be spared and protected by a Germany-led EU. This indicates that these wars will be different, and that Edom-Turkey in the End Times will not be allied with the radical Muslim countries of Iran, Iraq, Egypt or Syria, but will rather join with a United Europe under Germany. This conclusion is based on Psalm 83:8, which says, "Assur (Germany) also is joined with them."

Regarding Richardson's treatment of the two wars of Psalm 83 and Ezekiel 38 and 39 as identical wars, it is so obvious that the prophets Asaph and Ezekiel speak of two very different events that have nothing in common. There is no need to provide an in-depth analysis and waste precious time and space to proving what has already been clarified by the words of the prophets and is easily understood by readers. Instead we will enumerate only the most important distinguishing features of these wars.

First of all, their timing is not the same. The war of Psalm 83 must precede the war of Ezekiel 38 and 39 because by destroying the evil confederacy of plotters, Israel would have finally expanded the Promised Land – with all its richness of oil and gas and other natural resources – to the prophesied Biblical borders and, what is most important, would have lived in peace, prosperity and security: "all of them dwelling without walls, and having neither bars, nor gates" (Ezekiel 38:11). Everybody knows that such conditions cannot be applicable to Israel today because it is surrounded by Arab-Muslim enemies dreaming of throwing all Jews to the sea and repossessing their God-given Land. During this war or towards the end of it, the Messiah will likely have been revealed and taken part in the execution of God's judgments. Because Obadiah's book is entirely about Edom's future, it says that the House of Jacob (Twelve Tribes of Israel) will destroy the House of Esau (1:18); and the Prophet Isaiah (11:11-14) confirms that Judah and Joseph made peace, united and together attacked Edom, the Philistines, Moab, and Ammon—these things can have happened only after the advent of the Messiah's coming (Ezekiel 37:19-22).

The motives of these wars are also different. If the murderous confederation of Arab-Muslim nations plotted to annihilate the Israelite people and their State "that the name of Israel may be no more in remembrance," the hordes of Gog and Magog will have had another well expressed reason to attack Israel: "To take a spoil, and to take a prey, to carry away silver and gold, to take away cattle and goods, to take a great spoil" (Ezekiel 38:12-13). The participants of these wars are not the same; they are totally different. Salus' position on these matters is very clear: "There are two differing judgments determined for two differing battles, and two differing divine purposes will be accomplished in the aftermath of each. Thus Psalm 83 and Ezekiel 38 & 39 cannot be the same war."

Richardson's followers are so heavily influenced by his prophetic expertise that they thoughtlessly repeat after him such nonsense as "these two wars could actually happen simultaneously or be one and same." They ignore the words of the Prophet Ezekiel who implicitly said that Gog would attack Israel in the time when its people live safely, "all of them dwelling without walls, and having neither bars nor gates" (Ezekiel 38:11). Yet, as we all know, Israel had to build a 430-mile-long (700 kilometers) and 26-feet-tall (8 meters) concrete wall in the West Bank. In the north, along the Lebanese border and in the northeast, along the Golan Heights, the 45-mile protective concrete fence features touch sensors, razor wire, motion detectors, infrared cameras and ground radar. The 150-mile boundary defensive fence is being erected between the Sinai and Negev deserts. The southern barrier around Gaza runs for 32 miles. When all the walls and barriers are finished, Israel will be almost completely enclosed by steel, barbed wire and concrete, leaving only the southern border with Jordan between the Dead and Red Seas without a physical barrier. Even this is not sufficient. Israeli military engineers are planning to fortify this border with Jordan too. "We have become a nation that imprisons itself behind fences," says one Israeli official. Former Prime Minister Ehud Barak expressed it more figuratively, saying that the State of Israel is a "villa in the jungle." The walls and barriers have helped to keep the terrorists away but have not stopped thousands of rockets and missiles from being fired by Hezbollah and Hamas militants into Israel. Israel is surrounded by sworn enemy-states that threaten its existence and aim for its destruction. By no means has Israel dwelt in safety; it has become a defensive fortress among "evil neighbors" (Jeremiah 12:14-17). Certainly such a situation does not correspond to the description of the prophet regarding the Gog attack on Israel, so we can firmly conclude that the Gog and Magog war will occur much later than the wars of Psalm 83.

Richardson's identification of Edom as southern Jordan and Amalek as southern Israel, and Salus' equation of Edom with the Palestinians and their tents of refugees are both incorrect and contradict the prophecy of Asaph. If one were to believe these authors, one may conclude that Jordan is not only the home of the children of Lot – Ammon and Moab – but also the home of the people of Edom and the Hagrites. Edom of Psalm 83 is a very different country, big and very powerful, a country of the latter days, which only the combined forces of Joseph will defeat, says the Talmud. You may have figured out that we are referring to the modern Republic of Turkey, the head of the former Ottoman Empire. At one point in his rebuttal of Salus, Richardson even substitutes Assur with Turkey (and Syria and Iraq), simply saying that mighty Assur of the future, which God designated to be the ruler of the world and a whip in His hands to chase the nations of Israel, is Turkey: "O Assyrian, the rod of my anger, and the staff in their hand is my indignation" (Isaiah 10:5). He treats Turkey as the main hero (Gog) in the wars of Ezekiel 38 and 39, which will lead the armies of Gog and Magog. Turkey for him represents the land of Magog and the nations of Gomer, Meshech, Tubal, and Togarmah. Again, he sticks with his famous dogma that if the nation(s) in ancient times occupied certain territory, in this case Turkey, it does not matter that after three millennia this nation moved out of the region (Turkey), identified by a different name and descent, and dwelled in the opposite end of the earth. For Richardson all of this is irrelevant, even the fact that modern-day Turkey represents a different race of people (the Semites of Edom), and that the descendants of Japheth (Gomer, Meshech, Tubal, and Togarmah) moved long ago and today represent distinct nations and geographies. In Ezekiel 38:3-6 enlisted six Japhetic nations, including Persia, and two Hammitic nations of Libya and Ethiopia. Richardson theory could not be further from the truth; it stands alone, isolated from the numerous Bible prophecies, and contradicts Scripture.

Many scholars are amazed by the fact that Ezekiel 38 and 39, in describing the wars of Gog and Magog (who, basically, are the descendants of Japheth) against Israel, do not mention the Semitic nations as participants in these military campaigns. There is no Edom (Turkey), nor are Ammon or Moab, Syria, Egypt or Saudi Arabia, all of Semitic stock, mentioned. Do you wonder why? Because these Semitic nations who "plotted with one consent" against Israel in Psalm 83 will have been soundly defeated by the Israelites with the help of the Almighty on account of their aggressive and murderous deeds.

The Bible testifies that Israel executed the judgments of God towards Edom-Turkey a long time before Gog's hordes invaded Israel. This judgment was so severe that "there shall not be any remaining of the house of Esau," so how could Turkey as Edom be a member of the Gog coalition? Psalm 83, Isaiah 11:13-14, and Zechariah 12:6 and 14:12, speak of the prophesied defeat of those nations, which will occur before the wars of Gog and Magog—that is why the Arab Semitic countries will not be physically able to join Gog's hordes and that is why their names were not mentioned in the prophecies of Ezekiel 38 and 39. God knows precisely how the events of the future will transpire according to His divine master plan. And now is the time to reveal one of the most important Biblical "secrets," which is the key to unlocking and properly understanding the prophecies of Psalm 83 and the future development of geo-political events in the light of the Scripture, and that is the wars of the kings of the north and south recounted in Daniel 11:36-45. An entire chapter is devoted to this subject so as to offer a comprehensive explanation.

CHAPTER I

DR. ERNEST L. MARTIN

Three thousand years ago the Prophet Asaph listed the ancient nations according to their names at that time and their then-known geographical locations. Since we accept the notion that Psalm 83 is intended for the "last days" or "end of time," it is only common sense to assume that, after the passing of thousands of years, the names and dwelling places of these people have cardinally changed. Josephus Flavius, the celebrated Jewish-Roman historian, described this phenomenon in his work *Antiquities of the Jews*, chapter VI, saying that the ancient names of the nations after the flood significantly changed in many cases. Thus, Gomer, the first son of Japheth, founded people called Gomerites, but the Greeks changed their name to Galatians (or Galls). The Gomerites were the ancient Cimmerians and dwelled on the Eurasian Steppes, in southern Russia, Crimea, and Ukraine.

Magog, another one of Japheth's sons, founded the Magogites, but the Greeks renamed them Scythians. Flavius says that the Greeks called Scythia "Magogia." They also moved out of their ancient place in Anatolia to southern Russia and represent 60 million people of the Islamic "stan" republics. Solid historical accounts point to Magog being in Russia. This makes sense in light of Gog coming from the "far north" (Ezekiel 39:2). Turkey is out of equation because its geographical location from Israel is not from the "far north." Tubal (Thobelites) and Meshech (Mosocheni) were changed to Iberes and Cappadocians respectively. Elam, son of Shem, founded Elamites, but the Greeks called them Persians. However, there are some ancient names whose original names and places have not changed over the course of several centuries, such as Ethiopia (or Cush). The Egypt of Josephus's time was also recognized by the name Mizraim.

The late historian and theologian Dr. Ernest L. Martin (1932-2002) wrote of this phenomenon. He divides the history of humanity into four periods of time based on the ancient names and geographical movement of the nations: The first period represents the dispersion at the Tower of Babel to the Exodus of the Israelites from Egypt (22nd to 15th century BCE); the second period spans the Exodus of the Israelites out of Egypt to the Babylonian captivity of the Jews (15th to the 6th century BCE); the third period marks the Babylonian captivity to the conquests of Alexander the Great (6th to 3th century BCE); and the fourth period constitutes the time of Alexander the Great to the End Times generation. During the millennia of human development, some nations completely disappeared due to racial differences, wars, prosecutions, natural calamities, mortal disease and other determining factors; the others became known under different names, and most of them changed the places of their dwellings. One cannot find the names of modern countries, such as America, Turkey, Germany, Russia or China in Scripture. There is nothing unusual here. We know that all humans descended from Adam and Eve and later from Noah's three sons, Shem, Japheth, and Ham (Genesis 10), so with proper knowledge of the Bible, bloodline ancestry, and historical records we can trace the names of ancient people to the realities of the modern age.

Dr. Martin gives an exhaustive explanation of this process through the example of the Japhetic people. After the flood and dispersion at the Towel of Babel, most of the sons and grandsons of Japheth moved to southern Europe (Spain, Portugal, Greece, Italy), parts of Asia Manor (Turkey), islands (Cyprus, Rhodes), and other adjacent regions. All of these places were called by their names. Javan normally identifies with Southern Europe, sometimes only with Greece; the same goes for his brother Elishah. Kittim is connected to Italy, Cyprus and parts of Asia Manor. Togarmar (Tegarma, Tilgarimmu, and Takarama) is the third son of Gomer. He moved out of Anatolia and first settled in modern Spain and Portugal, then moved out and inhabited the area between the Black and Caspian Seas and founded the nations of Armenia and Georgia as well as some Turkic nations. The Khazar records say that Togarmah is regarded as the ancestor of the

Turkic-speaking people. In the time of the Prophet Ezekiel (c.622 BCE-570 BCE), Togarmah, together with his uncles Tubal, Javan and Meshech occupied the territory of Anatolia. There were Anatolian kingdoms called "Tegarama" by the Hittites and "Til-garimmu" by the Assyrians. Of all the theories concerning the nations involved in the Gog and Magog coalition of Ezekiel 38:2-6, the most probable is the so-called "Russian Theory," because in the opinion of many historians and theologians Gog and Magog refer to Russia and its southern "stan" Muslim Republics of Kazakhstan, Kyrgyzstan, Uzbekistan, Turkmenistan, Tajikistan, and possibly the northern parts of Afghanistan. Magog is commonly identified with Central Asia.

In the time of Ezekiel, Meshech and Tubal were identified as the ancient tribes of Mushki-Moshi and Tubalu-Tibareni and associated with the area south of the Black and Caspian seas. Eventually they were pushed out of this area in the time of the great migration of the Semite people and moved to the north (where they founded the city of Moscow) and east of Russia (where they founded the city of Tobolsk). The other descendants settled in southern Russia. There is the city of Tbilisi in Georgia, which very close resembles the name Tubal.

After the demise of the Assyrian Empire and the fall of its capital Nineveh in 612 BCE, many vassal nations found themselves free of Assyrian domination and began mass migration out of the troubled regions of Levant, Mesopotamia and Asia Manor northward and eastward, colonizing first southern and then central Europe. This mass exodus of Semitic nations such as Edom, Elam, Moab, and Ammon also included Assyrians, Babylonians and Israelites (the Ten Tribes), with some Jews who wished to remain in the Diaspora. "It is not uncommon for people to give a name to a region and then the original people move on to other areas or are killed off," explains Dr. Martin. That is exactly what happened to Japheth's descendants. Semitic people, together with the masses of other migrant nations, moved all over Europe, pushing Javan, Elishah, Kittim, Tarshish, Gomer, Tubal, Meshech and the rest of the Japhetic people to the extreme north (Evenks, Nenets, Eskimos-Aleut and other people of Ural, Siberia, Mongolia and so on) and east into most of the areas of Asia (China, Indonesia, Japan, Korea and many countries of Southeast Asia). Thus, Tubal became an eastern Mongolian people. Javan was no longer associated with Europe and his descendants became the Javanese people of the Southeast Asian area of Indonesia. Gomer, Togarmah, Javan, and Kittim left Europe and went into the central areas of Asia and particularly to China where they settled and gave their name to the region. In the writings of the medieval traveler Marco Polo and the Persian astronomer Nazir al-Din-al-Tuzi in 1272 we are told that China was known to outsiders by the names "Cathay," "Kitai," "Cataya," "Cathayan," "Khitayns," which very closely resemble the name of "Kittim." Many historians think that Japheth was "the father of the Indo-European people." Meanwhile, according to Dr. Martin, Japheth is "the father of yellow race people" whose population is the largest among the descendants of Ham and Shem. No wonder that God blessed Japheth with such "enlargement" (Genesis 9:27).

There is a fascinating theory expounded by Paul Phelps in *Oriental Origins in the Bible* and Ken Kwok in *Biblical Origins of Chinese People*. Both authors assert that East Asian mainland peoples are entirely Semitic and may be identified in Biblical terms as *Eastern Hebrews*. According to the Biblical list of nations (Genesis 10), the Hebrew race descended from the progenitor Eber who had two sons, Peleg and Joktan (10:25). They produced two branches of Hebrews. The students of the Bible are more familiar with Peleg's descendants because this line leads to birth of Abraham, Isaac, Jacob and David. Through these patriarchs we learn the whole history of the Israelites. The line of Joktan is not as popular or known. Despite the fact that this line is the most populous – Joktan begat thirteen sons – the Scripture mentions it twice (Genesis 10:26-30 and I Chronicles 1:19-23). The Bible is silent on the subject of the nations they constitute and the exact places of their dwelling. But here and there we can find hints that shed light on the mystery of Joktan's descendants. Thus, Genesis 11(1-2) informs us that before the Lord scattered people from the Tower of Babylon in the land of Shinar, all nations dwelled in the East and spoke one language.

Phelps and Kwok say that all of biblical history is based on Peleg's linage. But the descendants of Joktan made up another, even larger branch of Hebrews. The authors suggest that Joktan's people did not migrate from the east together with the house of Peleg to build the Babylonian Tower and did not take part in rebellion against God. It is known that the Hebrews of Peleg's line lived in that region because the Bible says that Abraham's family dwelled in Ur of the Chaldeans (Genesis 11:31). The line of Joktan preferred to go to the Far East and settle there. This separation of the two clans divided Hebrew people into the *Western* Hebrews of western Asia and the *Eastern* Hebrews of eastern Asia. The conclusion of scholars is that the East Asian mainland peoples (China) are entirely Semitic and may be identified in Biblical terms as Eastern Hebrews. The Hebrew descendants of Joktan founded China. Because these people were not affected by the Babylonian chaos, they kept the ancient original language brought over by Noah from Eden. The Semites of Joktan were not the only ones who settled in China. The Hamites and Japhethites settled there too. That is why China is composed of 56 ethnic groups. In the Bible, there is a prophecy referring to the future ingathering of the House of Israel from the nations of the world, even from the land of China: "Behold, these shall come from far: and, see, these from the north and from the west; and these from the land of Sinim" (Isaiah 49:12).

Too many interpretations of "the land of Sinim" have been given. Some say that Sinim means "south" and refers to Phoenicia; others say that it refers to the children of Canaan of the wilderness of Sin or Egypt of Sinai, south of Idumea. There are people who are convinced that Sinim is Australia, which was effectively hidden from the world until the voyage of Captain James Cook in 1776 ACE. But most scholars agree that the "land of Sinim" is China located in the Far East. This view of Sinim suits a context which requires a people to be "from far" and distinct from those "from the north and from the west." In fact, the nouns "Sinology" or "Sinologist" use the same root word "Sin," meaning China.

Enough theorizing about the origins of China; let us to return to the main subject of our narrative, which is Psalm 83 and its correct interpretation. When the majority of the Middle Eastern nations of Edom, Moab, Ammon, Israel, and Assyria moved out of the region, their places were taken by the victorious Median-Persian Empire (650-330 BCE). It became the ruler of the vast territories spreading from the Balkans to North Africa, Central Asia and the Middle East. Over the passing centuries and subsequent conquests, the Middle East passed from one Empire to another: the Persians were replaced by the Greeks, then the Romans, then Byzantine, followed by Arab Muslims and the Turkish Ottoman Islamic Empire. Some of those nations may live in close proximity to Israel, even sharing common borders, as with most of those listed in Psalm 83; others may be found at far away distances, such as Edom and Assur—a reality confirmed by Dr. Martin and many other scholars. If one disregards this situation and tries to identify those nations by their previous geographical areas, as Richardson or Salus do, one will misinterpret and twist the prophecy, and even nullify the essence of it—no matter what modern race or culture of people now reside in these lands. Yet that is what exactly many theologians have done with the prophecy of this psalm.

CHAPTER II

AN INTERPRETATION OF THE NAMES OF THE NATIONS IN PSALM 83

Edom

Let us begin with 'the tabernacles of Edom' (Psalm 83:6). All kinds of interpretations are given of the tabernacles, including the version that identifies today's Palestinian refugees as the tents of Edom, which fits perfectly with Asaph's vision. "Although the Palestinians are made up of a mish mash of ethnicities, many of them are Esau's Edomite descendants," states the renowned Christian theologian Bill Salus in his article "The Two End Time's Judgments Upon Edom."

On the surface this statement seems correct. But if one starts digging into the history of the Palestinians, one finds that there was no nation called by this name before the Six-Day War in1967. These people were the Arabs from Syria, Jordan, South Arabia, Iraq, Egypt, and Libya who recently immigrated to Palestine in pursuit of a better life. They shared Arabian history and culture, spoke the Arabic language, worshipped the same Allah, and proudly called themselves Arabs of Greater Syria, Jordan, Lebanon and so on. Never in history was there a Palestinian state in the land of Israel and these people have nothing in common with the ancient Canaanites, Philistines, Assyrians or Edomites. The name of the land "Palestine" was not known until the Romans, during the time of Emperor Hadrian in the aftermath of suppression the Bar Kokhba Revolt of (132-135 ACE). In 1912 Jews composed 64% of the population in Jerusalem, and the majority of the rest of the population was Christians. Palestine has never belonged to Arabs. Some prominent learned Palestinians have said: "There is no such country as Palestine. 'Palestine' is a term the Zionists invented. There is no Palestine in the Bible. Our country was for centuries part of Syria. 'Palestine' is alien to us. It is the Zionists who introduced it'" (Auni Bey Abdul-Hadi, Syrian Arab leader to British Peel Commission, 1937). Similarly, the Arab historian Philip Hitti asserts in 1946, "There is no such thing as Palestine in history, absolutely not."

In February 1919, the First Congress of the Muslim-Christian Association in Jerusalem adopted the following resolution: "We consider Palestine as part of Arab Syria, as it has never been separated from it at any time. We are connected with it by national, religious, linguistic, economic and geographical bonds."

The Palestinian leaders have built for themselves a new identity for purely political reasons, in order to legitimize their claim for land and justify Arab occupation of the Land of Israel: "There are no differences between Jordanians, Palestinians, Syrians and Lebanese. We are all part of one nation. It is only for political reasons that we carefully underline our Palestinian identity that serves only tactical purposes. The founding of a Palestinian state is a new tool in the continuing battle against Israel" (Zuhair Muhsin, military commander of the PLO and member of the PLO Executive Council).

As a matter of fact, before the Zionists settled the land of Israel, according to eyewitnesses, "The area was under populated and remained economically stagnant until the arrival of the first Zionist pioneers in the 1880's, who came to rebuild the Jewish land" (The report of the British Royal Commission, 1913). Similarly, Mark Twain observed in his travel writings that, "There is not a solitary village throughout its whole extent; not for thirty miles in either direction ... One may ride ten miles hereabouts and not see ten human beings. A desolate country ... a silent, mournful expanse ... a desolation ... We never saw a human being on the whole rout ... Hardly a tree or shrub anywhere. Even the olive tree and the cactus, those fast friends of a worthless soil had almost deserted the country ... Palestine sits in sackcloth and ashes ... desolate and unlovely" (Mark Twain, "The Innocents Abroad," 1867).

The Kingdom of Edom was in existence from the 14th century BCE to the 6th century BCE. Its territory consisted of the mountains extending from the Dead Sea in the north to the Red Sea in the south. On the west of Arabah the northern boundary of Edom is determined by the southern border of Israel (Numbers 34:3). The Edomites conquered this land from the Horites whose inhabitants were destroyed (Deuteronomy 2:22). The royal cities of Edom were Bozrah and Teman. During the period of the Second Temple the Edomites, under attacks from Nabateans and other desert tribes, began moving from their territory of southern Transjordan into southern Judea, and their kingdom became known as Idumea. Towards the end of the second century BCE (circa 109), John Hyrcanus conquered Idumea and forcefully converted its inhabitants to Judaism (Josephus, Antiquities of the Jews XIII: 257). In Roman time Idumea became part of the province of Judea. With the fall of Judea under the Romans, Idumaea disappeared from history after 70 ACE. There is even the false view that the Edomites no longer exist as an identifiable nation or ethnic group, that all the prophecies about them were fulfilled in the past (Isaiah 34; Jeremiah 49; Ezekiel 25, 35, Obadiah 1), and therefore all future prophecies concerning their punishment are void because it is impossible to punish a people who disappeared from the face of the earth millennia ago (Malachi 1:3).

From ancient times the Edomites had a tendency to heavily intermingle with other people as the life of their patriarch Esau amply manifested. Among his wives were Canaanite, Hittite, Ishmaelite, Hivite, Kenazite, Amalekite, and Horite women. Tiny portions of the descendants of Edom may be found among Jews, Moabites, Ammonites, Aramaeans, Ishmaelites, Amalekites, Phoenicians, Assyrians, Palestinians and many other people. In Rabbinical literature, Edom became associated with Rome in time. The Edomites were divided into the Twelve Tribes with an enormously large population, similar to the social structure of the Israelites or Ishmaelites. Not all the Tribes of Edom remained in their kingdom on mount Seir. Not all of them became the Idumaeans southeast of Judea and converted to Judaism. As the theologian Gavin Finley says, the Edomites, like many other groups of people, have migrated to different geographical locations. They are no longer found within their ancient borders. Even though communities and nations are no longer located within their ancient borders, it does not mean that they have disappeared from history. It seems that God has seen fit to hide this truth for the present. Some scholars affirm that the Edomites are "the Palestinians" or "the Arabs." Finley thinks that this is "sloppy scholarship." Bible scholars who make such assertions are highly presumptuous. Their claims do a disservice to the Arabs, he says in article "The Edomites Today."

The Arabs are not Edomites. God blessed Ishmael with wealth. The multitudinous population of the Twelve Tribes of 175 million people was promised a wonderful future. These people are the richest on earth, thanks to 5.3 million square miles of oil-rich land (compared to Israel's 8,000 square miles—a ratio of 662 to 1). Even their national character was determined: "Ishmael will be a wild man; his hand will be against every man and every man's hand against him" (Genesis 16:12). This prophecy characterized the Arab people as having an impulsive and violent nature. As history attests, they have continuously been involved in endless wars among themselves, as well as against Jews and Christians. There will never be lasting peace in the Middle East as long as there are fanatical Muslim Arabs who have no tolerance for the other people and religions practiced in the Middle East. Although they will face God's Judgment as "evil neighbors" and enemies of His people Israel, the Arabs' future is still hopeful. God Almighty has given them a choice: "If they learn well the ways of My people and swear by My name, saying, 'As surely as the LORD lives'– even as they once taught My people to swear by Baal – then they will be established among My people. But if they will not listen, then I will uproot that nation, uproot and destroy it," declares the LORD (Jeremiah 12:14-17). It seems that the Palestinians (the Philistines and Amalekites) are not going to correct their evil ways and accept the Almighty God of Israel, and by refusing to listen to Heavenly advice, they chose a destiny of destruction. No wonder that Scripture calls these people "a foolish nation" (Deuteronomy 32:21).

The Israelite and Arab peoples came from the same Semitic stock, from the same ancestral father Abraham. They are brothers, and should live together in happy brotherhood as peaceful neighbors. We think that it is Islam that is the root of the problem. It is Islam that divides the two nations and makes them sworn enemies. Hatred, lust for revenge, bloody wars—all are the products of Islam. It is not a battle between Jews and Arabs, as the international media tries to make us believe. It shows the Arab-Israeli conflict as an inherently irreconcilable struggle between Jews and Muslims, and Judaism and Islam, adding that the only way to engage in this struggle between "truth and falsehood" is through Islam and by means of jihad, until victory or martyrdom. This is not only a struggle for territory. This is a conflict of civilizations or, which is more correct, the war of civilization against barbarism represented by militant Islam and its pre-medieval caliphate. The real battle is between Judaism and Islam. Judaism does not intend to conquer and convert the entire world. Islam does. Judaism does not teach violence, terror, death. Islam does. Judaism does not avenge itself against the nations for not accepting their God, Torah and Prophets. Islam does.

One of the dogmas of Islam that prevents the peaceful coexistence of Palestinians and Israelis is the underlying teaching of the Koran that any land captured by Muslims cannot be given back to infidels, even if they were the lawful owners. This doctrine originated with Muhammad himself, as if it was Allah's command to never give up sacred Muslim territory and to fight for it until victory or martyrdom. This is the reason why the Arab Muslims of Palestine have rejected the two-state solution and are most reluctant to sign any peace agreement with the Israelis. The people of Israel (in their mind) have been cursed by Allah and are doomed for destruction. The Koran compares Jews to monkeys and apes. The Islamic religious leaders, and particularly the Palestinian Authority, have continued educating its population to hate Jews and to want them dead. Their children, instead of playing baseball and learning arts and crafts in summer camps, are taught how to shoot weapons and kill Jews. Their television and radio shows constantly appeal for the destruction of Israel. They encourage suicide bombers and especially value and glorify those who kill the most of the Jews. They name streets and town squares by the names of those "heroes," whom they proudly call "Shahid," that is, a martyr, one who dies deliberately for the Islamic faith. The Muslim religion is categorically against any Jewish presence in the land of Israel, and fundamentalist Muslims may never quit their jihad-like struggle until the last Jew is killed, or they are soundly defeated and dispossessed off the land. They declare that this century will be "The Century of Islam" because "there is no god but Allah" and explain that the Islamic messianic age will not come unless there is a mass slaughter of the Jews. They even specify that, "We are not talking of killing Zionists only. Let's not mention Zionists. The Jews are our enemy and, please God, we should finish them all." According to S. Spykerman, these statements were made by Muslim fundamentalist scholars at the Islamic University conference in London in 1994. They hate the Western world, especially the USA, as well. That is why the population of

Gaza and the West Bank wildly cheered and danced on the streets as thousands of Americans were murdered by the militant Islamists during the 9/11 terrorist attack in New York City. Their leaders condemn the USA for killing Osama bin Laden whom they praised as a holy warrior of Allah.

Islam claims that the Prophet Muhammad's revelation from Allah was the final one and supersedes the Jewish and Christian religions. Thus, Ishmael has replaced Isaac as Abraham's heir and Muhammad has replaced Moses. And, of course, they have rejected all the blessings God pronounced upon Isaac and his descendants and abrogated them for themselves. This is another variation of Islamic "Replacement Theology." Militant Islam is like a growing cancer that attacks the most vital parts of the body; to ensure the peace and security of the world, this evil cancer must be removed before it is too late.

There are few voices of dissent among the Muslims with the strength and courage to tell the truth. One such voice belongs to Sheikh Ahmad Adwan, a Muslim scholar from Jordan. He says to the Palestinians that their claim to the land of Israel is invalid: "There is no such thing as 'Palestine' in the Koran. Your demand for the land of Israel is a falsehood and it constitutes an attack on the Koran, on the Jews and their land. Therefore you won't succeed, and Allah will fail you and humiliate you, because Allah is the one who will protect them (i.e. the Jews)." Sheikh Adwan witnessed human rights abuses by the Palestinian Authority and brutal sacrifices of the civilian population in times of war or confrontation with the Israelis: "The Palestinians are the killers of children, the elderly and women. They attack the Jews and then they use those as human shields and hide behind them, without mercy for their children as if they weren't their own children, in order to tell the public opinion that the Jews intended to kill them. This is their habit and custom, their viciousness, their having hearts of stones towards their children, and their lying to public opinion, in order to get its support." This 'habit and custom' is precisely what the Palestinians are practicing today in the Israeli-Gaza conflict.

The other Muslim supporter of Israel is Imam Dr. Muhammad Al-Hussaini of England, who believes that the return of the Jews to the Holy Land and the establishment of the State of Israel are in accordance with the teachings of Islam. Sheikh Al-Hussaini states, "You will find very clearly that the traditional commentators from the eighth and ninth century onwards have uniformly interpreted the Koran to say explicitly that *Eretz Yisrael* has been given by God to the Jewish people as a perpetual covenant. There is no Islamic counterclaim to the Land anywhere in the traditional corpus of commentary." Such Muslim Zionists are rare and have faced vehement opposition and violence from the majority of the Muslim world.

There is only way to stop the ancient hatred and bloodshed in the Middle East between the Arabs and Jews (and between the Arabs and the rest of the world) and establish true peace among the nations, and that is for militant Islam to be rejected as the false, hateful and idolatrous religion of the god Allah who cannot save, and to turn to God Almighty, the one and only God, who can save, the God of Israel: "And the Lord shall be King all over the earth: in that day there shall be one Lord and His name one" (Zechariah 14:9). It is up to the Arab nations to choose destruction or life. All they have to do is turn and pray to the God of Israel that He may forgive their wickedness that they and their children may live, as it is written, "If at any time I announce that a nation or kingdom is to be uprooted, torn down and destroyed, and if that nation I warned repents of its evil, then I will not destroy it as I had planned" (Jeremiah18:7, 8). The ultimate triumph of the God of Zion is envisioned by the prophets: "It shall come to pass in the last days that the mountain of the Lord's house shall be established in the top of the mountains; and all nations shall flow unto it. And many people say, come you to the house of the God of Jacob; and He will teach us of His ways, and we will walk in His path; for out of Zion shall go forth the law, and the word of the Lord from Jerusalem" (Isaiah 2:2-3). Idolatry will be utterly abolished by God for ever. "Look unto Me, and be you saved, all the ends of the earth: for I am God, and there is none else. Unto Me every knee shall bow, every tongue shall swear" (Isaiah 45:22-24). The God of Israel personally calls upon all the nations of the World, including the Arabs, to reject idolatry and wickedness and turn to Him to be saved. Turn! Turn you from your evil ways; for why will you die, O House of Ishmael?

Not so with the Edomites—the terrible judgment of God awaits them. They hate God and Israel, and they never repent. By their own actions they doomed themselves. Those Edomites, who mixed with the nations surrounding Israel and disappeared, were an insignificant minority. The vast majority of the Edomites split into different groups and moved from the area to various places of the world (Europe and Asia) as the Israelites did long before the fall of the kingdom of Seir and even became partners with the Assyrians in the time of the defeat of Israel and their subsequent exile by the Assyrians. Edom closely participated with the Philistines of Gaza and Phoenicians of Tyre during the Assyrian conquest of Israel, helping to catch Israelites attempting escape and delivering them into the hands of Edomites and Assyrians (Amos1:6, 9). For hunting and shedding the blood of the children of Israel by the force of the sword in the time of its calamity, for acting revengefully in anger and wrath against its brother, and casting off all pity, God will send a fire upon Teman, make its cities desolate, and destroy its people (Amos 1:11; Ezekiel 35:5; Obadiah 1:10, 18).

According to the historian Dr. Herman Hoeh in *The Compendium of World History*, the Edomite kings were rulers of Persia and Turkmenistan and these regions became known as "the Land of Temani." The Bible says that kings in the land of Edom reigned before the appearance of the kings of Israel (Genesis 36:31). It was the great King Husham of Edom who ordered Moses not to cross his territory on the way to Canaan, and the children of Israel wandered in the Sinai Desert for forty years. In the eleventh century ACE the Edomites (Turks) left Central Asia and Turkmenistan and settled in Turkey.

While it may be admissible that all the surrounding Israel enemy-nations, of mainly Arabic stock, comprise the elements of Edom, Ishmaelites, Moabites, Ammonites, Hagrites, Philistines, Amalekites, Phoenicians, and Ottoman Turks, Edom of the Prophet Asaph is not rightly identified and so far is absent from this prophesy. As shown on a few occasions elsewhere, the Palestinians are the Arabs who recently (120 years or so) immigrated to Palestine from the Arab countries surrounding Israel to pursue economic opportunities. In 1934 alone, approximately 33,000 Arabs left the Hauran Province in Syria for a better life in Palestine, where the Zionists provided jobs and improved medical, educational, and other services.

The significance of Edom is demonstrated by the fact that it appears first on the list of nations conspiring against Israel. One cannot compare the military prowess of the Palestinians of the West Bank (or their "tents of refugees"), identified as Edom by many theologians, with that of Syria, Egypt, Jordan or Saudi Arabia—the countries so easily labeled by scholars as members of this confederacy. The Edomites, in the manner of other nations, migrated to various geographical locations. They are no longer found within their ancient borders of Palestine or Mount Seir. Some people suggest that the tabernacles of Edom include the nations of Rome-Italy, Germany, Turkey, Spain, Mexico, and so on. The Palestinians of the West Bank, together with their "tents of refugees," are not Edom of Psalm 83:6. "If we can believe what God has written by His Holy Spirit in our Bibles, the Edomites are not only present in the end-time drama but they will come to their doom at the end of the age," says Gavin Finley. We should look for another Edom, large and powerful, that could win the war against Judah and "break his yoke from off thy neck" and free himself from his brother's domination of the past, as the prophesy predicted (2 Chronicles 28:17; Genesis 27:40).

Such an Edom is well illustrated in the prophetic Book of Obadiah. These prophecies were written for the End-Times. We will not trace and discuss all of the descendants of Edom throughout Europe and Asia in order to maintain the scope of our narrative. Instead, we will focus on Teman, a son of Eliphaz, the firstborn of Esau who ultimately settled in Turkey and after whom the Ottoman Turkish Empire was named: "And thy mighty men, O Teman, shall be dismayed" (Obadiah 1:9). Yes, Edom-Turkey will be a key player in the upcoming events.

The Greek historian Strabo wrote of the two related tribes of Odomantes and Edoni dwelling in Central Asia. The Ottomans descended from the Odomantes. The ruling family of Turks was called "Osman," which comes from the Turkish name "Othman." Othman was the founder of the Ottoman dynasty. These Ottoman Turks descended from the Odomantes or the Temani of Edom. According to J.M. Roberts in *The Penguin History of the World*, "these Osmani Turks are the "Oghuz" Turks. A descendant of Husham was Alphidun who had two sons, firstly Tur, who ruled over the Edomites in Central Asia" (360-61, 372-73 ACE). This may be the origin of Turkestan. *The Encyclopedia Britannica* says that there are two branches of Turks: the western and eastern. The western group from southwestern Asia settled in Anatolia (Turkey). The eastern Turks inhabited Kazakhstan, Turkmenistan and other regions in southern Russia and China. There are many varieties of Turkic people, but western Turks are predominately white and generally of the Caucasoid race known as Ogus Turks. Of the date and circumstances of the descendants of Teman's move to their new homeland of Turkey, the *Britannica* explains that western Ogus Turks known as "Seljugs" migrated into Iran and created a new Empire under the sultan Alp-Arslan (1063-72). In 1071 ACE he defeated the Christian Byzantine Empire at the Battle of Manzikert and thereby opened the way for several million Ogus tribesmen to settle in Anatolia (modern Turkey). These Turks came to form the bulk of the population there, and one Ogus tribal chief, Osman, founded the Ottoman dynasty (14th century). This was the most significant migration of the Turks into Anatolia. The Ogus are the primary ancestors of the Turks of present-day Turkey. The Ogus are not identical with the eastern Turks because their original homeland was not in Central Asia.

Edward L. Winkfield and Samuel C. Baxter explain that a clue regarding the Oguz Turks can be found in the name "Ottoman." This name was adopted from the ruler Osman, whose name is also spelled as Othman and Uthman. Edward Gibbons cited the other variations of "Thaman" and "Athman," whose Turkish name has been melted into the appellation of the caliph Othman (The *Decline and Fall of the Roman Empire*). No matter how you slice it, all the evidence point to the Biblical Teman, the grandson of Esau. The Esau-Eliphaz-Teman descendants gave rise to the Ottoman Turkish Empire, which we know today as modern Edom-Turkey.

The land of Turkey lacks natural raw materials and resources. The Anatolian Plateau of Turkey accounts for 97% of the country's area. It consists of virtually inaccessible hills and rocky mountains unfit for agriculture. It is a barren stony land. It is important to remind the reader that the land of the previous dwelling of Esau in his kingdom on mount Seir was not much better. In the rugged mountainous region, fertile land was in short supply. This description corresponds with the prophetic blessing Esau received from his father Isaac: "Your dwelling will be away from the earth's richness, away from the dew of heaven above" (Genesis 27:39).

Why would Teman settle in Turkey? What could possibly attract him to this land? First of all, it is a transcontinental country that lies in a strategically important geographical location at the juncture of two continents—Europe and Asia. Surrounded by water on three sides, Turkey shares well-defined natural borders with eight countries. Turkey stands as a bridge between Western and Islamic civilizations. It is situated in Anatolia in Western Asia and in the Balkans in Southeastern Europe, bordering the Black Sea, between Bulgaria and Georgia, and bordering the Aegean Sea and the Mediterranean Sea, between Greece and Syria; Georgia is to the northeast; Armenia, Iran and Azerbaijan are to the east. The Sea of Marmara, the Bosphorus and the Dardanelles – the Turkish Straits – separate Europe and Asia. From ancient time, this Middle Eastern territory was the junction of trade routes connecting Europe and China, India and Africa and the rest of the cultures of the Mediterranean basin. These trade routes were known as early as five thousand years ago. The Edomites' relatives – the Hittites – with the Phoenicians of the eastern Mediterranean traded olive oil, figs, coffee, lemons, lentils, pomegranates, and spices. The cedar trees of Lebanon were of plentiful supply and good quality as they were prized above all other trees. Their pine wood was always the first choice for building temples and palaces. The well-traveled Eurasian Silk Roads, which flourished during the Byzantine Empire, were a very profitable enterprise for Edom-Turkey. China traded not only silk, but also many valuable products such as gunpowder, paper, and oranges to the Mediterranean world. Along with goods the Silk Roads transported people, ideas, art, science, philosophy, and religion. The trade routes were the communication highways of the ancient world.

The Edomites of Turkey are the descendants of those ancient Edomites who had already enjoyed the benefits of trade with other nations in the past (1200 BCE), when they lived in their kingdom on mount Seir. Their land also lay at the crossroads of the Silk Road from China through Persia and Arabia and the Incense Route, which was controlled by the Arabs, who brought frankincense and myrrh by camel caravans from Saudi Arabia. The Edomites controlled the trade routes of Egypt, Arabia, Syria, and Mesopotamia. They collected tolls from merchants for passing through their territory, supplied them with camels and donkeys, provided inns and food for people and animals, and assumed the responsibility of policing the trade routes. Their largest city, Petra, on the fringes of the Syrian Desert, grew rich providing services to merchants and acting as an international marketplace. All of these commercial activities greatly contributed to Edom's wealth. In addition to the many territorial benefits of Turkey, Teman offers a superior refuge to the homeland of his grandmothers, Adah and Basemath – the Hittites – whom the grandfather Esau married at the age of forty against the will of Isaac and Rebekah, his parents (Genesis 26:34). The Hittites were an ancient people who dwelled in the center of the Anatolian plateau and had their mighty empire in the capital city of Hattusas, which lasted for roughly 800 years (c.2000 BCE-c.1200 BCE). The borders of their kingdom included north-western Syria and upper Mesopotamia. It is Adah the Hittite who bore Esau's first-born son Eliphaz, from whom came Teman and his four brothers who are all called in the Bible "the sons of Adah Esau's wife" (Genesis 36:4,10-11).

It should be remembered that the prominence of Teman as a patriarch of the Edomites in Scripture is understood in the same way as the prominence of Joseph among the Israelite Tribes. When the name "Teman" mentioned, it is applied to all Edomites (Amos 1:12; Obadiah 1:9; Jeremiah 49:20), as the name "Joseph" is a metaphor of the Ten Tribes of Israel in exile (Ezekiel 37:16). Edom of the Prophet Obadiah is a huge and powerful entity, very proud of its achievements and arrogance of power. The Prophet Ezekiel condemned the nation of Edom, saying, "Thou hast had a perpetual hatred, and hast shed the blood of the children of Israel by the force of the sword in the time of their calamity" (Ezekiel 35:5). Throughout ancient history, the Edomites manifested their hatred against the Israelites, as demonstrated by their refusal to grant permission to Moses and his people to pass through Edomite territory (Numbers 20:14-22). They joined the attacking forces of Babylonians under Nebuchadnezzar in 586 BCE and took an active part in capturing and killing the Hebrews and destroying Jerusalem and the Temple: "Remember, O LORD, the sons of Edom in the day of Jerusalem, who said, 'Raze it, raze it, even to its very foundation'" (Obadiah 1:11; Psalm 137:7). For the grievous sins of Edom, for rebellion against God and outrageous pride of heart, the Almighty will bring him "down" to earth, and make him "small" and "despised" among the nations (Obadiah 1:2-4). These verses indicating the future punishment of Edom in the End-Time are corroborated by the prophets of the Bible. The Edom of Psalm 83:6 is definitely not the Edom of the Palestinians of the West Bank or their refugees dwelling in tents. When they stated that in the future only Joseph would be able to defeat the powerful forces of Edom, the sages of the Talmud clearly did not mean that this dangerous and mighty enemy would be identified with the so-called the Palestinians. It is Esau who was blessed by God to be a strong and skillful military power who would, with his descendants, dominate the nations and "live by the sword" (Genesis 27:40). Turkey has done precisely that and is well qualified to be Edom. "The tabernacles of Edom" is incorrectly understood as the tents of Palestinian refugees. There is a much better and more trustworthy explanation that identifies the real descendants of Teman as representatives of the modern Republic of Turkey, whose army would have joined the confederate armies of Psalm 83 and pitched their tents of war close to the borders of Palestine in anticipation of the attack against Israel. Bill Salus admits that the people living in tents may well represent the military encampments from the Biblical point of view.

Some authors and the sages of the Talmud identify Edom with the ruling classes (elements), nobles and aristocracy of European countries such as Italy, Germany, Japan, Austria, Spain, Hungary and others. We will elaborate on this identification later in connection with the process of identifying the mysterious Assur of Psalm 83:8. There are scholars who would not even bother to search for the physical descendants of Edom by bloodline, DNA or race, saying that it is not physicality or biology that is important, but the Edomite spirit of thinking, feeling, and acting. Any person of any race, by their criteria, may become an Edomite by adopting the Edomite spirit of evil. The Edomites were crushed by the Babylonian armies in the 6th century BCE, and then the Nabateans drove them from their mountain fortresses of Mount Seir into the Negev desert to the west. In the time of Hyrcanus, the High priest and ruler of Judea, the remaining Idumaeans were conquered and converted to Judaism. Later on, the Edomites were finally destroyed together with the Jews by the Roman general Titus during the First Great Jewish Revolt of 66 to 70 ACE. In short, such scholars state that all the prophecies of Edom's punishments have been fulfilled, and there is no reason to apply them to the future because the Edomites are no longer in existence.

There are authors who suggest that Edom is represented by modern Spain. To make their theory appear valid, they describe the cruelty of the Spanish Inquisition during the Middle Ages as "the worst and most atrocious blood-bath and bestial religious persecution of all time" directed against Jews. Forceful conversions and the expulsion of the Jews in 1492, great hatred for the Jewish people and vicious persecutions— all these facts point to the Edomites who have been noted for their extreme hatred of and cruelty towards the Israelites. "Is not this persistent hatred a manifestation of the ancient hatred of Esau for his brother Jacob?" rhetorically asks one of these authors. To illustrate that their identification of Edom as Spain is supported by the Biblical prophecy of Edom "dwelling far from the fatness of the earth and of the dew of heaven from above" (Genesis 27:39), such authors describe the land of Spain as agriculturally impoverished, with poor soil, lack of natural resources, and limited rainfall making it difficult to grow crops.

Some people say that the Edomites are Arabs and identify the Palestinian Arabs with Edom in Psalm 83:6. This is a common tendency among many scholars. However, there is no Scriptural or historical basis for such an assumption. The well-known theologian Gavin Finley calls this "sloppy scholarship." The progenitor of the Arabs was Ishmael. Esau was the father of Edomites. Both these nations are very distinct and in existence today. The Arab world includes all the Arabic speaking countries of North Africa, Southwest Asia, and the Arabian Peninsula. The Edomites of Turkey are linguistically dissimilar from Arabs because they do not speak the Arabic language and they are not Arabs. They belong to the Islamic world by religious affiliation, but to a different nation by bloodline. Iran, Afghanistan, Pakistan, and Indonesia are also Muslim countries, but are not made up of Arabs, even though they make up the Islamic world. Of course, it does not mean that countries such as Iran and

Turkey do not have a large minority of Arabs. Regarding the Edomites, their country's name is the Republic of Turkey. The descendants of Esau are reputedly the most hairy people in the world as was their patriarch. They moved into the region of Turkey and created the Ottoman Empire with its capital of Constantinople—one of the most powerful Empires in the world. The Khazars called the Byzantium Emperor in Constantinople the "King of Edom" because they were so familiar with the origins of the Edomite people. At its peak, this brutal and arrogant power controlled Turkey, Greece, Bulgaria, Romania, Hungary, Macedonia, Egypt, Israel, Jordan, Lebanon, Syria, North Africa, and parts of Arabian Peninsula. In the aftermath of WWI the Ottoman Empire was finally conquered in1917 by the combined forces of England and America—the descendants of Jacob. Again, these facts of Edom's origin have nothing to do with the Palestinians and would not qualify them as the wise and intelligent men that the prophets describe as the Edomites (Obadiah 1:8; Jeremiah 49:7), not even taking into account their "military prowess." The Edomites were famed for their wisdom, excellent writings and art (Jeremiah 49:7; Baruch 3:22). Many Turkish sultans were renowned for their wisdom, such as Suleiman the Magnificent. One of Job's friends was Eliphaz the Temanite, the oldest and wisest man (Job 2:11). Their military skills and power are detailed in the Bible: "By the sword shall you live" (Genesis 27:40). Their Ottoman Empire ruled many nations for more than five hundred years and was in possession of huge territories, including Palestine. The Edomite leaders emerged as talented men of war and won many battles during WWI, but were ultimately defeated by the forces of Joseph.

The wrath of God will be directed against the inhabitants of Teman from the north, as well as against Dedan, which is in the south: "I stretch out My hand upon Edom; and I will make it desolate from Teman; and they of Dedan shall fall by the sword" (Ezekiel 25:13). At the sound of their fall the earth will tremble. Despite its great influence and importance, the Almighty will make Edom the smallest and most despised among the nations (Jeremiah 49:15, 21). This prophecy was partially fulfilled in 1917, when the allied forces of Joseph defeated the vast, powerful, and brutal Turkish Ottoman Empire and it disintegrated.

The Empire lost its great status, and was stripped of most of its non-Turkish possessions, including land and people. It became the small country known as Turkey, the "Sick Man of Europe," despised and hated for its barbarian past. The destiny of Edom-Turkey is clearly outlined in this prophecy: "I will lay My vengeance on Edom by the hand of My people Israel, that they may do in Edom according to My anger and according to My fury; and they shall know My vengeance," says the Lord God (Ezekiel 25:14). Israel will finally deliver itself from Edom forever (Obadiah 1:16-18). All these terrible events will not happen in the land of Palestine, but in the land of Edom where the inhabitants of Teman are dwelling:

"For the Lord Almighty will offer sacrifice *in the land of the north by Euphrates River*" (Jeremiah 46:10, emphasis added). Palestine is not located near the river Euphrates. This river rises from eastern Anatolia, flows southward through southeastern Turkey, goes across the border into Syria and Iraq, and empties into the Persian Gulf. Its length is approximately 1800 kilometers, of which 971 are in Turkey.

In another place the Scriptures say, "The earth is moved at the noise of their fall, at the cry the noise thereof was heard in the Black sea" (Jer. 49:21). God has never said that He will destroy the Holy Land of Israel (which is called Palestine by the pro-Arab world) and make it uninhabitable forever. But that is what He says of the land of Teman (Edom): "For my sword shall be bathed in heaven: behold, it shall come down upon Edom, and upon the people of My curse, to judgment. Their land shall be soaked with blood, and their soil made rich with fat. And the streams of Edom shall be turned into pitch, and her soil into brimstone; her land shall become burning pitch. Night and day it shall not be quenched; its smoke shall go up forever. From generation to generation it shall lay in waste; none shall pass through it forever and ever" (Isaiah 34:5, 9-10). And more: "I will deal with you; you shall be desolate, Mount Seir, and all Edom, all of it. Then they will know that I am the Lord" (Ezekiel 35:1-15). The prophet is not only speaking of the previous destruction of the Edomite Kingdom on Mount Seir; his words are also directed at "Edom, all of it." There would be no need to use these words if the rest of the descendants of Edom had not existed. Here is the link to Teman-Turkey. These facts alone should have warned B. Salus and J. Richardson against identifying Edom in Psalm 83 with the regions of Palestine or southern Jordan.

All the prophets have predicted that the land of Edom will be destroyed as a punishment from God: "As in the overthrow of Sodom and Gomorrah and its neighboring cities, says the LORD, no man shall abide there, neither shall a son of man dwell in it" (Jeremiah 49:18). This is another reason why the land of Israel, where the so-called "Edom-Palestinians and their refugee tents" live, cannot be compared to the future destruction of the land of Edom-Turkey, and that is why the Palestinians cannot possibly be identified as the Edom of Psalm 83:6.

There is another description of Edom's land which may help us to locate the country of Teman: "Thou should not have entered into the gate of my people in the day of their calamity ... Neither should thou have stood in the crossway, to cut off those of his that did escape" (Obadiah 1:13-14). The prophet, according to the commentaries of Bible scholars, depicts a country of extremely significant geostrategic importance whose location is at the crossroads of Europe and Asia, and that controls Dardanelles, formerly known as Hellespont, a narrow strait in the northwest linking the Aegean Sea with the Sea of Marmara. The other strait in this country is Bosphorus. Both of these straits are international waterways that connect the Black Sea to the Mediterranean Sea and serve as a land bridge between Europe and the Middle East. So, what country in the world fits all of the criteria of this description? The answer is obvious: the prophets, and especially Obadiah, speak of the modern-day Muslim Republic of Turkey as the land of Edom and the country of the Edomite people of Teman, the grandson of Esau, the son of his firstborn, Eliphaz. Teman was one of the most important "dukes" of Edom and his name is used as a synonym for Edom itself (Genesis 36:15, 42; Amos 1:12; Obadiah 1:9). As mentioned by the theologian Yair Davidiy, Esau was red and hairy. From an anthropological point of view, the most hirsute people in the world are the Turks. The early Turks were described by others as red-haired. Later they intermixed with other peoples and largely lost this quality, which is interesting because there are those who identify the Turks with Edom.

To properly understand the participants in this bloody coalition – that is, which nations will take part in the crusade against Israel and which will not – readers must understand an utterly surprising future reality. Before the events of Psalm 83 and the Gog and Magog wars of Ezekiel 38 and 39, there will be another war in the Middle East as outlined in detail by the Prophet Daniel. It is of interest to note beforehand that the ten nation confederacy against Israel described in Psalm 83 is not mentioned in Ezekiel's account of the Gog and Magog wars, but most of these nations will be active participants in the preceding wars of the king of the north against the king of the south recorded in Daniel's prophecies (Dan. 2:40-45; 7:7-8, 23-24; 11:40-45). We discuss these wars later on, when Assur of Psalm 83:8 will finally be accurately identified.

CHAPTER III

IDENTIFYING ASSUR: SYRIA OR IRAQ?

Let us now discuss the identity of Assur in Psalm 83: "Assur also is joined with them" (verse 8). Many theologians (Bill Salus and Joel Richardson, for example) equate Assur with Syria, Iraq or Turkey. Obviously, there is no country in existence today by the name of Assyria. Why would they come to the conclusion that Assur will represent these countries in the End Time? The progenitor of the Assyrian people was Assur, son of Shem. The Syrians originated from Aram, son of Shem, and were also called Aramaeans. From these brothers came absolutely distinct nations, as with Isaac and Ishmael or Jacob and Esau. One thing is generally held in common among these nations—centuries-old hatred of Israelites. It is perplexing that the names of the worst enemies of Israel, such as Iran, Iraq, Egypt, and Aram-Syria, are not mentioned in Psalm 83.

The Arab Islamic conquest in the mid-seventh century ACE established Islam in Iraq and saw a large influx of Arabs and also Kurds. The first Arab kingdom outside of Arabia was established in Iraq's Al-Hirah in the third century. During the rule of the Ottoman Empire, the nomadic population of Iraq swelled with the influx of Bedouins. The dominant group in Iraq is the Iraqi or Mesopotamian Arabs, who comprise three-quarters of the total population (including the Palestinians). The minority groups consist of Kurds (17%), Turkmen (3%), as well as Persians, Armenians, Assyrians, Circassians, and Mandaeans. Iraq is a Muslim country in which Islam accounts for 97% of the citizens. In 1920 the League of Nations, under British mandate, created the State of Iraq, which consisted of a Sunni minority and a Shiite-Arab majority.

During the rule of the Ottomans the population of Syria was also multiracial. There were the religious minorities of Shia Muslims, Greek Orthodox Christians, Maronites, Armenians, and Kurds. The predominant language of Syria is Arabic but there are others languages spoken as well: Aramaic, Kurdish, Armenian, Circassian, and Turkish. In 1920, the League of Nations, under French mandate, turned Ottoman Syria into the short-lived Arab Kingdom of Syria, a name that signaled its predominately Arab population. In 1946, Syria became independent. Modern-day Syrians are commonly described as Arabs, with a majority consisting of Sunni Muslims (74%) and a minority of Alawites (11%). There are also Christians of various backgrounds and denominations who are connected to Arab culture, history, and language. How can the immensely diverse people of Syria and Iraq be identified with Assur, which is neither a Muslim nor an Arab nation?

In his work "Germany in Prophecy," Dr. Herman Hoeh writes: "When the ancient Greek writers wanted to distinguish the Assyrians from the Aramaeans or Syrians, the Greeks called the Assyrians *Leucosyri,* meaning 'whites' or 'blond' as distinct from the very brunette Syrians who still live in Mesopotamia." Remarkably, this description is still valid today when one compares the color of the Syrian or Iraqi people of the Middle East to the Assur-German people of Deutschland. Although racially and culturally similar, Assyrians are distinct linguistically, physically, and for the most part, geographically from the Syrian Christians of Syria.

According to the historically supported theory of Dr. Ernest Martin, the Assyrian Empire partially comprised the territories of Syria, Iraq and Turkey and ruled many countries and nations of the region. After the collapse of their Empire, the Assyrian people migrated northwest to Europe together with the other Semitic nations of the war-torn Levant and Mesopotamia. The Assyrians and hordes of other invaders pushed the descendants of Japheth further north and east by means of wars and then settled in Europe. The fact that the Assyrians occupied the land of Syria, Iraq or Turkey in ancient time by no means makes them Syrians, Iraqis or Turks of today. The Prophet Asaph was not interested in the geography of the nations. He knew that geography would not change but more or less remain the same. His prophecy concerns the particular nations in the latter days that will despise Israel and build a confederacy against it, regardless where they are located. Some of those nations will be in close proximity to the borders of Israel, such as the Ishmaelites, Moabites, Ammonites, Amalekites, Gebal, Tyre, and Philistines; others will be as far away as Turkey and Germany with the ten kings of the European Union.

To say that Assur will be Syria or Iraq in the End time is misleading and scripturally incorrect. There are many prophecies in the Bible concerning Assur of the last days, which means that Assur is the Assyrian people, not the Edomites, Elamites, Medes of Persia, Aramaeans of Syria, or Mesopotamian Iraqis. They are not Arabs, Aramaeans or Kurds. Their religion is not Islamic. And their language is not Arabic. When the Bible speaks of Syria in the End times, it does not substitute the Syrian people for other nations and tribes, including the Assyrian people. Although there is the similarity of the names and territories, one should not be confused by it, because the Syrians and Assyrians are different people.

Syrians today are, as they have always been, the offspring of Aram, the patriarch and founder of the Aramaean people. Despite occupying land similar to ancient Assyria, the origins of these two nations is not equivalent, and they are absolutely distinct nations, now living in different parts of the world. They have a different ancestry, history, culture, language, and religion. Israel, too, was descended from Arphaxad, the brother of Assur and Aram, but that does not automatically makes Israelites Syrian or Assyrian people.

Aram and Assur are given different roles in the Biblical prophecy for our age. The destiny of Syria is outlined in Isaiah (17:1, 3). Damaskus is taken away to be a city. It will be completely destroyed, "a ruinous heap," never to be rebuilt and left uninhabitable. Assur will endure multiple punishments from God: "Thy shepherds slumber, O king of Assyria. There is no healing for thy bruise ... All that hear the bruit of thee shall clap their hands over thee: for upon who hath not thy wickedness passed continually?" (Nahum 1:14; 3-all). Assur, the mortal foe of Israel, will threaten and even invade the country again. Here is another blow to the proponents identifying Assur with Syria and Iraq, for Assur is identified in these prophecies as the country of the north (Jeremiah 6:22) who will attack Israel in the future and be terribly punished by God (Isaiah 10: 5-6, 24-25; Daniel 11:45).

One cannot change the name of the nation under the pretense that another nation in the far removed past conquered and ruled it for some period of time. Israel and Judea were also defeated and ruled by the other nations, but nobody calls Israelites or Jews by the names of Assyrians, Babylonians, Persians, Greeks or Romans. The same goes for Assur—the Bible means what it says. Otherwise, those who erroneously substitute the name with other nations willingly deny the existence of Assur today and distort the prophecy.

CHAPTER IV

ASSUR TODAY

The first time we read of Assur is in Genesis, where it says that the father of Asshur was Shem, son of Noah (10:22). From his brother Arphaxad – an ancestor of Abraham – come the Israelite people. The Israelites and Assyrians are kindred people. Assur means "leader," "successful," and "powerful."Assur had four brothers: Elam (Sumerian, or Akkadian, in ancient times; today Croatia, Serbia, Poland), Arphaxad (ancestor of Abraham from whom the Twelve Tribes of Israel came), Lud (the people of Anatolia, Lydia), and Aram (the father of Aramaeans, now called Syrians). The celebrated Judaeo-Roman historian of the first century, Josephus Flavius, writes that, "Ashur lived in the city of Nineveh; and named his subjects Assyrians, who became the most fortunate nation, beyond others" (Antiquities I, 6:4). Assur was the father of the Assyrians and the country was named after him. He was regarded as "the great god, king of all the gods." The Bible regards him as the founder of Assyria. The Assyrian civilization began its existence in the late 25th century BCE as a Semitic Akkadian kingdom and lasted until 612 BCE when a combined force of Babylonians, Meads, and Scythians destroyed the Assyrian army and captured the capital city of Nineveh, thus bringing an end to the independent Assyrian Empire. So what happened to the Assyrian People after the defeat and collapse of their Empire? Have they disappeared from the face of the earth without a trace? Or, do they still exist as identifiable people with a distinct history, culture, language and religion?

There is a huge popular misconception concerning the Assyrian people. Encyclopedias and other historical sources correctly instruct the public that the Assyrian people are still in existence today. Historians explain that the Assyrians did not migrate anywhere after their defeat by the Babylonians, Medo-Persians, and Scythians and the fall of their capital Nineveh in 612 BCE, but remained a political entity under the rule of various empires until the seventh century ACE, when their empire dissolved and they gradually became a minority in their homeland. Their numbers in the world today are estimated at between 3.5 to 4.5 million. They are scattered in small communities all over the world, and have never had their own state or any measure of autonomy. Most of them dwell in Iraq, Syria, Turkey, and Iran. They are Semitic people by race and the direct descendants of their ancient predecessors— the Akkadians and Sumerians. Their history spans over five thousand years. They speak their own common Assyrian neo-Aramaic language. From the beginning of the Common

Era the Assyrians adopted the Christian religion, but follow many rival churches, such as the Assyrian Church of the East, the Chaldean Catholic Church, the Syriac Orthodox Church, and the Syriac Catholic Church; they are similarly split among different political affiliations. Prior to Assyrians' conversion to Christianity, the religion was Ashurism, after the Assyrian god Ashur whom Assyrians worshipped as a deity. In the modern era their ancient territory is the north of Iraq, part of southeast Turkey and northeast Syria.

After the Assyrian genocide by the Turkish Ottoman Empire during WWI, the Simele massacre in Iraq (1933), the Islamic revolution in Iran (1979), Saddam Hussein's persecutions and Kurdish nationalist policies, as well as the killings of Christians by the Muslims revolutionaries of Egypt, Lybia, Iraq, Sudan, and Syria, during the recent Arab Spring the Assyrian people began to migrate from their homeland to North America, Europe (Germany, Sweden, and France), Australia, New Zealand, Lebanon, Jordan, Armenia, Georgia, and Israel. Despite the persecutions and massacres, as well as enormous pressure from the Muslim world, the Assyrian people refused to be converted to Islam or to be culturally or linguistically Arabized.

These facts are pivotal points in the history of the Assyrian people. Do they align with the Scriptural description of Assur? Do the Assyrians of today resemble Assur as prophesied in the Bible? Unfortunately, the answer is emphatically in the negative. The people whose history was just recounted could have belonged to an indigenous Assyrian population because it consisted of many tribes and ethnicities, such as the Ishmaelites or Israelites; however those Assyrians may in no way be substituted with the Assur of End time prophecies. How could those small communities of so-called Assyrians who live all over the earth, without state, army, or influence in world affairs, constantly persecuted and always on the run—how could they fulfill the prophecies of our age as a mighty and powerful Empire capable of being "rod of My anger" (Isaiah 10:5-7) in punishing Israel and dominating the other nations? How could those insignificant people, small in numbers, fit the prophecy of Nahum (1:14; 3-all) that describes the joy of the nations after the awful destruction of Assur and the king, "for upon whom hath not thy wickedness passed continually?" Those few peaceful Christ-loving Assyrians could not have been people who perpetually committed evil and terrorized the world, upon whose terrible demise the nations happily 'clap their hands.' The prophecy also speaks of the King of Assyria. What does it mean? The king has to rule. It implies that the king possesses the country, kingdom or dominion. These conditions are certainly not applicable to the now small, scattered, and persecuted people without a homeland of their own.

But there is such a country and a mighty nation in the Bible that perfectly fits the visions of the prophets: "Behold, a people comes from the north country, a great nation. They shall lay hold on bow and spear; they are cruel, and have no mercy; their voice roars like the sea; and they ride upon horses, set in array as men for war against thee, O daughter of Zion" (Jeremiah 6:22-23). This country should be a new super power: "their kingdom shall be strong as iron: forasmuch as iron breaks in pieces and subdues all things: and as iron that break all these, shall it break in pieces and bruise" (Daniel 2:40). Assur of Psalm 83 could not possibly correspond to the Christian Assyrians with whom we are preoccupied, because this Assur is a strong and respectful entity joining the confederacy in the war against Israel under the false pretense of helping Moab and Ammon, the children of Lot. The Prophet Balaam foresaw the future of Assur: "And ships shall come from the coast of Chittim and shall afflict Assur" (Numbers 24:24). This verse speaks of the future destruction of Assur. That this event will happen in the days to come confirms the vision of the Prophet Daniel: "But tiding out of the east [Chittim-China] shall trouble him (Daniel 11:44). Both passages speak of the same events and involve the same entity: Assur. In the second instance, Daniel speaks of the king of the north who has been identified as modern Germany, the leader of the Common Market of Europe (e.g. the EU). Yes, there are many verses in the Bible that speak of Assur of the End Times as a world power to be reckoned with. Once more, as in ancient times, Assyria-Germany will rise to greatness and dominance. The Bible says that it will be its last time. There are some authors who wonder that, and cannot understand why, there is no nation called Assyria at present, but Psalm 83 says that Assur will be a mighty nation and will join the Arab-Muslim coalition to see Israel defeated. To trace the ancient Assyrians to modern times is as important as finding the lost Ten Tribes of Israel.

So, if those Christian Assyrians of the history books do not fit this mighty Assur of the latter days whose importance and might are often emphasized in prophetic visions, who, then, is this mystical Assur? Through research Assyria (Assur), an ancient Semitic race, can be accurately traced to the modern people of Germany! Germany is the king of the north of Daniel's prophecy. The German people are the descendants of the ancient Assyrian people. What evidence could lead to this conclusion? Plenty. Remember when the Assyrian people 'disappeared' in Mesopotamia after the fall and destruction of their capital Nineveh in 612 BCE? This event, as it were, took place at approximately the same time that the Germanic tribes appeared in Europe. These Germanic tribes, according to the testimonies of contemporary historians, were called Assyrians. There is no evidence that the Assyrian nation as a whole was assimilated and absorbed by the victorious Babylonian, Median or Persian peoples. As a matter of fact, such a series of events by no means took place.

There was no mysterious disappearance of the Assyrian nation. Historians mark this period of time as one of great human migration. Where did the Assyrians go after their defeat? For the answer to this question, let us refer to the eyewitness historian Sylax of Caryanda (550 BCE), the author of the *Periplus*, who wrote that, "The coast of the Black Sea is called Assyria." According to the Greek historian Diodorus, who was writing between 60 and 30 BCE, Assyria was a large colony in northern Asia Minor south of the Black Sea. Is there any confirmation of this claim? Yes, indeed: "A warlike people called the Assyrians inhabited the North of the Black Sea," wrote the Roman historian Pliny the Elder (23-79 CE) in *Natural History*. He also located an Assyriani tribe, as he called it, among the Scythian people in Crimea north of the Black Sea.

As we can see, from the time of Sylax who documented the Assyrians on the south side of the Black Sea, to the time of Pliny the Elder, the Assyrians have migrated over vast expanses of land, moving not only to the north of the Black Sea, but also much further to the center of Europe, to the shores of the Rhine river. The people of the former mighty Assyrian Empire, together with their vassal nations, including the Ten Tribes of Israel (the heavens and history have tied Assur and Israel to the End times to fulfill the prophecy), traveled the same well-established route between the Black and Caspian Seas northwest into Europe.

At the same time that the Assyrians "disappeared," the ancestors of the Germans emerged in the precise area of the Black and Caspian Seas. Was that a coincidence? The Roman Emperor Julius Caesar (60 BCE) and the historian Tacitus (98 CE) did not think so when they called those tribes living along Rhine "Germanii," meaning men of war. Tacitus was sure that the Germans came from their original home in Asia Minor. It is he who informs us of the German habits of early morning washing, wearing loose flowing robes, and tying long and braided hair in a knot on the top of the head—practices which must have been of eastern origin. In *The Great German Nation: Origin and Destiny* C. White says that this particular German hairstyle "seems similar to the Assyrian hairstyle."

Many medieval Arab historians were of the opinion that the Assyrians were of similar ethnicity as the Germans and originated from the same source. They identified this source as Nineveh and Persia. Jerome the historian (347-420CE) said that the "descendants of Assur" were among the Celtic-Scythian-Hun people then invading Europe and confirmed that, "Assur (the Assyrian) is also joined with them along the Rhine." Incidentally, the words of Jerome – "Assur is also joined with them" – resemble those of Psalm 83; in fact, they are identical. Jerome was one of the first historians who identified Assur of Europe with one of the Indo-Germanic tribes that originated in Mesopotamia. "There can be no doubt that they [the Germans] immigrated to Europe from the Caucasus and the countries around the Black and Caspian Seas," as Smith records in *The Classical Dictionary* (36). These sources strongly suggest that the origin of Germany is ancient Assyria. Herbert W. Armstrong in his work *Mystery of Ages* (*1985*) concludes: "The Assyrians settled in central Europe, and the Germans, undoubtedly, are, in part, the descendents of the ancient Assyrians." Of the same opinion was Herman L. Hoeh in his *Compendium of World History*, published in 1963.

The Germans do not like to call themselves by that appellation. They would prefer to call themselves "Deutsch," and their country—"Deutschland." The early legends of Germany often mention the name "Tuysco" or "Tuisco," sometimes called "Tuisto" or "Tuitsch." In *The Origin of the Germans,* published in 1605 ACE, Richard Verstegan, publisher and antiquarian, claimed that Tuysco was "the first and chiefest man of many among the Germans, and after whom they do call themselves Tuytshen, that is, Duytsches or Duytsch people." According to historian Tacitus's account in *Germania*, Tuisto was a deity among the Teutons and the first person who sprang from the earth. The Germans often spell the name Tuysco as Tiw or Tyr in the same manner as they pronounce the name Asshur.

Johannes Turmair (1477-1534 ACE), the Bavarian Renaissance historian, wrote in *The Bavarian Chronicle* in 1526 that Tuitsch or Tuisto reigned from 2214 BCE to 2038 BCE and was the son of Noah. His other son Mannus would have been the father of Trebeta who, according to legend, built Trier. Trebeta's father was the Assyrian King Ninus. Thus Ninus and Mannus were the same person—Mannus would have been merely the German name for Ninus. This means that Ninus or Mannus was identical to Asshur, and that Asshur's father Shem, the son of Noah, was none other than the German Tuitsch or Tuisto. The Germans of old worshiped a pantheon of pagan gods. Their chief god was Tieu, the god of war, known as Thur or Thor. These names resemble the name of the Assyrian god Assur. In ancient manuscripts Assur is often referred to as Athur or Thur, and the country of Assyria is repeatedly designated as Athuria.

This explanation can be found deep in history of the Germans' predecessors, the Assyrians. Asshur was the supreme god of the Assyrians, who later became known according to the shorter form of Tyr or Tir. As noted in *The Encyclopedia Britannica,* the Assyrians of old called their land "Athur," which is an Indo-Germanic form of the Semitic "Asshur." In Germany Athur is known as Tyr or Tiw.

They are the gods of war, victory, and heroic glory and associated with courage and combat. Tyr and Tiw are the other names of Asshur. Since Asshur or Tyr was the Assyrian ancestor and god, it is of no surprise that the "Germanii" in Europe, who were migrated Assyrians, have continued the same tradition, calling their deity Tyr or Tiw. Whenever a German calls himself Deutsch, he is saying that he is Tiw's or Asshur's son—an Assyrian. And when he calls his country Deutschland, he is saying that it is Tiw's or Asshur's land— that is, Assyria.

CHAPTER V

ASSYRIA AND GERMANY

There are striking similarities between ancient Assyria and modern Germany. These similarities can be easily found, and they are neither far-fetched nor imagined. No other countries in the world are so uncannily alike. The parallels between German and Assyrian cultures are obvious and unique—consider German and Assyrian history and language, love and glorification of war, domination of other people, perfectly organized and centralized governments, thoroughly militarized societies, well-equipped and brutally efficient armies, strong Hattian influences, practices of cruelty, genocide, mass-scale deportation and slave labor, attitudes of Arian superiority, appetite for conquering weaker nations, and ambitions of global imperialism. No other nations fit this description so perfectly.

Scientific linguistic analysis shows that both Assyria and Germany have spoken an Indo-Germanic language. Both Assyrians and Germans are war-loving cultures called "Germanii" by the Romans, meaning "men of war." The

Germans are known for their tendency to break treaties in the same way as their ancestors, as the following examples attest: The Treaty of Versailles, signed between Germany and the Allied Powers in 1919 at the end of WWI, was violated by Germany more than once. In March 1935, under the government of Adolf Hitler, Germany introduced compulsory military conscription and began rebuilding the armed forces—actions strictly prohibited under the terms of the Treaty. In March 1936, Germany reoccupied the demilitarized zone in the Rhineland and in 1938 violated the Treaty again by annexing Austria in the Anschluss (political reunion).

Take the further example of the Molotov-Ribbentrop Pact. On August 23, 1939, Nazi Germany and the Soviet Union signed the Nonaggression German-Soviet Pact, in which the two countries agreed to take no military action against each other for the next ten years. Germany broke this pact in June 1941, and the Nazi forces invaded the Soviet Union.

"Not a single neighbor of the Germans could ever trust the Germans to remain peaceable. No matter how happy their condition, their restless passion would urge them on to ever more extreme demands," writes Emil Ludwig. Speaking of unparalleled cruelty of its predecessors, the Assyrians, this German author, in his book *The Germans: Double History of a Nation*, says, "The history of the German kings and leaders during the Middle Ages is a story of revolt and conspiracy … In matters of torture the Germans in the Middle Ages exceeded all other nations in inventiveness."

Margaret Thatcher, the former prime minister of England, characterized Germany this way: "German reunification was a big mistake for which all of Europe is now paying. Germany is very powerful now—her national character is to dominate. You have not anchored Germany to Europe, you have anchored Europe to a newly dominant, unified Germany. In the end, my friends, you'll find it will not work."

Of Germany's predecessor –Assyria – Leonard Cottrell wrote: "In all the annals of human conquest, it is difficult to find any people more dedicated to bloodshed and slaughter than the Assyrians. Their ferocity and cruelty have few parallels save in modern times." Indeed, in modern times Germany has been more dedicated to cruelty and bloodshed than any other nation. "German militarism and Nazism have devastated twice in our time generation the lands of German neighbors," says experienced American politician James F. Byrnes.

James McCabe, author of *History of the World*, says the Assyrians were a "fierce, treacherous race, delighting in the dangers of the chase and in war. The Assyrian troops were notably among the most formidable of ancient warriors ... They never kept faith when it was to their interest to break treaties, and were regarded with suspicion by their neighbors in consequence of this characteristic ... In organization and equipment of their troops, and in their system of attack and defense and their method of reducing fortified places, the

Assyrians manifested superiority to the nations by which they were surrounded" (Vol. 1, PP. 155, 160).

In his work *Germany in Prophecy,* Dr. Herman Hoeh writes, "Ancient Assyria was the greatest war-making power in all of history." The whole organization of the Assyrian state was centered around the military. For the first time in history the idea of centralization was introduced into politics. The Assyrian empire was the most powerful, terrorizing, cruel, and aggressive war machine of the ancient world. Its people loved wars. They were skilled, highly disciplined, and fearless warriors. This warring nation was merciless and cruel to their enemies. Extreme acts of cruelty and torture were essential characteristics of the Assyrians. They executed nobles and kings of captured enemies as public spectacles for their people. They mutilated bodies, plucked out eyes, cut off the tongues and ears, and stocked severed heads and corpses to intimidate and control their foes. As the history of Germany during WWII attests, Assur-Germany also practiced genocide, deported conquered nations on a massive scale to different locations of the Empire, and used forced slave-like labor for their interests. Like Hitler, the Assyrians enjoyed public parades with music and lights to demonstrate the grandiosity of their might and superiority of their race. Their empire was well organized and their army was very efficient. It consisted of chariots, cavalry, infantry, and engineers. Their desire to rule other nations, their insatiable war-lust, and inherent feelings of superiority towards other people—these were the national character traits of the Assyrian people. The Assyrian Empire was the largest in the ancient world. In 732 BCE it captured Babylonia and Syria; in 722 BCE the Northern Kingdom of Israel (Ten Tribes) fell into its hands; in 701 BCE it forced Judea pay tribute; in 671 BCE Egypt was defeated and became the vassal state of the Assyrians. The entire Fertile Crescent was under Assyrian control.

In West Germany, the ancient city of Trier (called Treves in English) lies on the banks of the Mosel River, on a border with Luxemburg. This city was founded circa 2,000 BCE by Trebeta, the son of the Assyrian king Ninus. An inscription that is still readable says that the Assyrian colony and the city of Trier were founded 1,300 years before Rome. As we know from history, Rome was founded in 753 BCE. Simple calculation leads us to believe that Trier was built at the time of Abraham. Ninus quite often identified with the Biblical Nimrod, the son of Cush, who founded Nineveh. This identification cannot be right because in Genesis 10:11 it is written that it was Assur who built Nineveh. The legend says that the King of Assyria married another wife by the name of Semiramis, who became the Queen and stepmother of Trebeta. After the death of Ninus, Semiramis took over the kingdom and made her son heir to the throne, thus bypassing her much-despised stepson. Trebeta left Assyria with a group of colonizers, went to Europe, and founded the city of Trier.

Germany's unexpected and surprising return on the world stage as a powerful economic and political leader of Europe is a miracle of itself. It is prophetically significant that, after being reduced to rubble at the end of WWII, Germany (Assur) rose from the ashes like the legendary Phoenix and become a European super power. If this had not happened, there would not have been the Assur of the Bible. There is no doubt that when the Bible mentions Assur in the End times, it is speaking of Germany.

CHAPTER VI

THE HITTITES

It was an ancient civilization that established the Old Hittite Kingdom at Hattusa in north-central Anatolia around 1600 BCE. The vast empire encompassed the territory of Asia Manor, northern Levant and Upper Mesopotamia. The Hittites were first people who learned to smelt iron which brought them economic prosperity. They valued iron five times more than gold and eight times more than silver. The Hittites were skillful warlike people with superior iron weapons who knew how to make successful use of chariots. The name "Chatti" or "Hatti," as it sometimes reads, means "to break down by violence or confusion; to abolish, make afraid, scare, or terrify" in Hebrew. This name was equally applied to the Hittites as well as to the Assyrians living among them.

Some historians suggest that the Hittites originated from the area of central Europe and northern Germany. They left Europe and entered Anatolia well before 2000 BCE. Their kingdom was destroyed by the Sea People, a group of Indo-European tribes of disputed origin who attacked much of the Middle East by land and sea around 1200 BCE. Sometime after 1180 BCE, the Hittite Empire came to an end, splitting into several independent city-states, some of which survived until 8 century BCE, when Assyria conquered them and gradually absorbed them into its society. The Hittites were heavy intermarried with the Assyrians, spoke the same Indo-European language, were absorbed by the Assyrians and significantly contributed to the ancestry of modern Germans. Those Hittites who settled in northern Syria were called "white Syrians" or, in the Greek language,—"Leucosyri." The Hittites together with other Assyrians became one of the Germanic tribes of modern Germany. Their complexions are predominately white or blond, and they have reddish hair and blue eyes. Sometimes this ancient people are called 'Chatti' but they claimed their descent from Hittites or Hatti. These people had many things in common with the Assyrians. They spoke the same Indo-Germanic language. Both nations loved war, and had very well-equipped and disciplined armies. Even their national symbol – a double-headed eagle – was the same and later reappeared in the cultures of Germany, Prussia, and Austria. These two nations were so closely interrelated that the Romans called the Hittite capital city "Ninus Vetus," meaning "The Old Nineveh." Meanwhile, as is well known, Nineveh was the capital city of the Assyrians. The main cities of the Hittites were Hattusas, Kussar or Kussara. Their kings were called "the kings of Kussar," supposedly giving birth, as some authors suggest, to the word "Kaiser," the Prussian and German word for "emperor." Some researchers go even further, insisting that from the Hittite's "Hatti-tsars" came the Roman emperors' title of "Caesar." The Hittites were linguistically and culturally linked to two of the German tribes—the Hessians and Prussians. Historians sometimes label the Hittites as the "Prussians of the ancient world," whose function was "to safeguard the civilized world against barbarian threats." During medieval times, the Holy Roman Empire under the domination of the Kingdom of Germany and its famous Emperors, undertook the similar function in Europe.

As is written in the Table of Nations (Genesis 10:15), the Hittites are ancestors of the Biblical Heth, a descendant of Ham through his son Canaan. Let us not forget that the people of Canaan and his descendants have been under a divine curse: "Cursed be Canaan; a servant of servants shall he be to his brothers" (Genesis 9:25). Some scholars contend that modern Germany may consist of the admixture of Semitic and Canaanite people. But there is another version of the Hittite's origin. James Hastings' *Dictionary of the Bible* of 1899 says that, "Besides the northern Hittites, other Hittites, or sons of Heth, are mentioned in the Old Testament as inhabiting the south of Palestine. These are the Canaanite Hittites of the line of Ham. It was them whom Abraham asked to sell the cave of Machpelah for Sarah's burial (Genesis 23:10-20). Many historians recognize that there were two different groups of people who called themselves Hittites, Hatti or Chatti. *The Encyclopedia Britannica* confirms this phenomenon: "The identification of the northern and southern Hittites, however, presents certain difficulties not yet fully explained; and it seems that we must assume Heth to have been the name of both a country ... and of a tribal population not confined to that country" (11ᵗʰ ed., vol. 13, article "Hittites"). *The Britannica* describes the Chatti as "an ancient German tribe" which "frequently came into conflict with the Romans during the early years of the first century" (vol. 6, article "Chatti"). Here you are—there existed the northern red-haired, fair-skinned blue-eyed Assyrian ("Leucosyri") Hittites and the southern dark-skinned brunette Hittites, the descendants of Canaan. Both these people were fierce and skilled warriors, cruel and efficient in their battles, who loved war and caused surrounding nations to tremble in fear and terror. If the Assyrian Hittites, the sons of Assur, migrated to central Europe and settled in the territory of Germany, the Canaanite Hittites, in the time of Alexander the Great, migrated "across the Atlantic to North America and became known as the Chatti Indians of the Central Plains," as suggested by Dr. Hoeh.

Historical sources indicate that the early inhabitants of Germany were the Hittites (Chatti), who were also called the Hessians. These names are identical; in fact, the Old German spelling of Hesse was Hatti. These people share much in common. The swastika, as a symbol of good luck and success, was widely used in Hittite society. The archaeologists discovered iron swastikas in the sites of Hittite strongholds and temples. Heinrich Schliemann (1822-1890), a German pioneer of field archaeology, connected the Hittites' particular shape of swastika with similar shapes found on ancient sites in Germany. He concluded that the swastika was a "significant religious symbol of our remote Hittite ancestors." The Hittites used it as a symbol of the master race. They demonstrated deep-rooted feelings of superiority over other nations. During the 1920s, the Nazi Party of Germany began using the swastika in a similar way: as a symbol of Aryan superiority, fascism, and racism. Some people called Adolf Hitler "Hitler the Hittite." For 3,000 years, the swastika was used as a symbol of sun, life, power, and good luck. The Nazis of Germany transformed it into a sign of racial superiority, hate, and death. The double-headed eagle was the symbol of the ancient Assyrian Hittites, and has become a symbol of Germany, which adopted irs predecessors' claim to be the distinctive Aryan race of an ideologically-motivated white master race and Nazism. The Hittites and Prussians shaped the history of modern Germany.

CHAPTER VII

EDOM AS GERMANY?

Many Bible expositors believe that Germany is Edom. Jewish tradition teaches that Israel is presently in the fourth and last Diaspora, which will immediately precede the arrival of the Messiah. This Diaspora is called the Diaspora of Edom, also known as the Roman Diaspora. According to tradition, it was the Romans who defeated the Jews, destroyed the second Temple and forcefully exiled the people of Judaea out of the Promised Land. It was also the birth and rise of Western Christian civilization with its culture, spirituality, morality, and ethics that led to the Jewish Diaspora. The sages of the Talmud have consistently identified the ruthless Roman Empire with the descendants of Edom. This notion is supported not only by the destruction of the Temple, by millennia of unspeakable persecutions, pogroms, Crusades, and Inquisitions, and by expulsions and murders, but also by their culmination in the Nazi Holocaust. The Romans behaved towards the Jews in the manner of their ancient enemies, the Edomites. That is why, in the minds of the sages, the wicked and cruel Rome was associated with Edom and Christianity. Rabbi Yehuda Lowe, who lived in the sixteenth century and was known as the Maharal, explained that the characteristics of ancient Jewish writings attributed to Esau-Rome may apply to Euro-Western civilization as a branch of the Esau-Rome tree. The eighteenth century Lithuanian rabbi Elijah ben Solomon Kramer, called the Genius of Vilna, confirmed the Maharal's opinion that half of the nations of the contemporary world are branches of the Esau-Rome genealogy.

The rabbis' conclusion is questionable because Edom-Germany does not fit into the prophecy. We have already established that the Edom of Psalm 83 is the modern Republic of Turkey. It is clear that this prophecy does not require two different Edoms. Prophet Asaph himself differentiates between the Edom of verse 6 and the Assur of verse 8, saying that, "Assur also is joined with them," making them two different entities. If they were both the descendants of Edom, it would make no sense to separate them as the Psalm does. Assur here is very different from the rest of the participants. It is evident that, geographically speaking, he does not belong to this group of nations. If he were one of them, there would be no need to speak of him separately and designate him as special. The prophet would continue the list of nations with the use of a 'comma' or 'and,' without using the meaningful word 'also,' indicating that Assur is treated here additionally as a respectful and strong ally whose presence may guarantee the victory of the plotters.

To illustrate the point, let us assume that Assur here represents Syria, as many theologians have suggested. Syria is the country located in close proximity to Israel on the northwestern border. The rest of the surrounding Israel nations listed in this prophecy border Israel from different directions, forming the countries of the "inner cycle." If Assur was Syria, the prophet would have written, "The tabernacles of Edom, and the Ishmaelites; of Moab, and the Hagarenes; Gebal and Ammon, and Amalek; the Philistines with the inhabitants of Tyre, *and Syria*." However, to emphasize the significance of Assur's participation in this confederacy, to show that this entity is very special militarily (as a mighty Empire) and culturally (as a different religion), and does not belong to the list of the regional nations mentioned in the prophecy, Asaph used the word "also." There is nothing special about Syria as Assur or the Palestinians with their "tents of refugees" as Edom to justify the application of this word. Nevertheless, B. Salus and other scholars believe that because Psalm 83 listed the tents of Edom first, the Palestinians will play a key role in this upcoming war. As for the rest of the nations of the "inner cycle," generally speaking they are not much different from each other; they are all Muslims and Arabs, share a common hatred towards Israel, and wish to obliterate it as a nation, and take over the Holy Land. None of these nations represent a mighty superpower that could become an authoritative and indisputable leader of a coalition.

What makes Assur-Germany different from the rest of this confederacy is the fact that Assur of old has transformed into a powerful Christian Empire cemented by the Catholic Vatican. Its main purpose in this military campaign, as it was in the time of Crusaders, is to recapture the holy city of Jerusalem, the cradle of Christian civilization, and to establish full control of the Middle East in order to secure hydrocarbon energies for its national interests. This Empire is located in Europe and calls itself a newly resurrected Holy Roman Empire, the rise of which was prophesied in Scripture as the fourth beast of the fourth kingdom (Daniel 7:7; 23-24). Germany, as the descendant of Assur, is the economic, political, and military leader of this Empire, nowadays called the European Union or Common Market of Europe. Assur as Edom in this prophecy simply makes no sense. But Assur as Germany makes a lot of sense. When Asaph prophesied that, "Assur also is joined with them," he knew that Assur would not join this confederacy of plotters against Israel single-handedly. All the prophecies of the Bible are connected and lead one who understands them to see the whole picture from beginning to end. The Almighty God does not do things without letting the prophets know His plan. Assur – the fourth kingdom of Daniel 7:23 – will join the confederacy of Psalm 83 with the ten kings-countries of the European Union Empire against the whole House of Israel.

That Assur is not Syria or Iraq is clear from many passages of the Bible. Thus the Prophet Isaiah says: "And there shall be a highway for the remnant of His people, who shall be left, from Assyria; like it was to Israel in the day that he came up out of the land of Egypt" (11:16). This is the prophecy of the future Israelites' return to the Promised Land. The remnants of God's people will not return from Iraq and Syria for the simple reason that they are not living there anymore because the Jews were forcefully exiled from these countries a while ago. The remnants of the Israelites, as the prophecy says, will return from Assyria – which represents the German-led Common Market of Europe – in the same manner as they came back from the land of Egypt. That we are on the right track in identifying Assur with Germany in connection with this prophecy is supported by the fact that the EU is full of people with Israelite roots, that is, descendants of Jacob. The prophecy speaks of these people and their return from Assyria (Germany).

Why would the prophet end his list of nations with the words "they have helped the children of Lot?" (verse 8). Who are "they?" Are they the nine nations, including Ammon and Moab (known as the children of Lot), listed before Assur? Ammon and Moab supposedly joined this coalition to help themselves, so are they the principal powers involved in the confederacy? What kind of help did they need and why? Are they the leaders and initiators of the planned attack on Israel? Are the rest of the countries merely their auxiliary helpers, including Assur? This scenario is unlikely and not supported by Scriptural analysis of the prophecy. Or perhaps these words apply to Assur-Germany together with the group of European nations comprising the ten allied kings? Yes, indeed. The real and decisive military leader here is Assur-Germany who alone will decide the time and the way that this campaign will be conducted.

What is the purpose of this plot of nations against Israel? It is clearly stated: "to cut them off from being a nation" (verse 5). Nevertheless, in verse 8 Asaph gave another reason: "they have become a help to the children of Lot." It seems that there are two groups of nations in this confederacy which pursue different goals. There are nine Muslim-Arab nations that are plotting to completely eradicate Israel from the face of the earth that "the name of Israel may be no more in remembrance." The other group of nations make-up the European Union under the undisputed leadership of Assur-Germany, whose main goal, as previously mentioned, is to recapture Jerusalem, secure national interests in terms of oil and gas from the Middle East, and establish a new world order under their hegemony. To kill or somehow eliminate the Israelites is not their priority, as is evident in Psalm 83. How and why Assur-Germany will join the coalition is another story to follow.

CHAPTER VIII

EDOM AND ASSUR

Some theologians and sages of the Talmud teach that Edom represents the ruling classes, military leaders, nobles and aristocracy of European countries such as Italy, Germany, Spain, Portugal and the other "non-Israelite sections of Europe." This opinion is widely disseminated within scholarly communities. But if this is the case, why would Psalm 83 list Edom – that is, the non-Israelite countries of the Common Market of Europe – twice: the first reference is erroneously interpreted by many scholars as "the Palestinians of the West Bank and their tents of refugees"; the second reference incorrectly views Assur as the Edom of those European countries. This makes no sense.

There is no need for two Edoms in this prophecy. Assur as Germany is different. It does not belong to these countries of the "inner cycle," bordering Israel. It is a mighty military power situated in Europe, able to "help the children of Lot" and to pursue plans to destroy the king of the south (Iran) and conquer its allies of Iraq, Syria, Egypt, Lybia, Ethiopia, and Jerusalem (Daniel 11:40-45). Besides, Germany as Edom or, in this case as Assur, would not join this confederacy of plotters against Israel single-handedly. The students of the Bible are well aware of the modern-day resurrection of the holy Roman Empire of Europe, also called the Common Market of Europe, (EU) under the political, economic, and military leadership of Germany, which is the fourth beast or the fourth kingdom of the prophecy, and will bring with him ten kings-nations (Daniel 7:23-24).

How may one speak of the fourth beast of the European Empire separately from its heart and soul, the organizer and undisputed leader— Assur-Germany? Is not something wrong here? If the Palestinians with their tents of refugees and Assur with its many European countries are Edom, then the prophecy of Psalm 83 would become completely nonsensical. Such an interpretation of the nations involved in "crafty counsel" against Israel definitely does not fit the Biblical description. It is one thing to regard Assur as a different entity than Edom in this prophecy; but to add that Assur in this confederacy serves the secondary role of equal ally and helper to Moab and Ammon in their military plot is another matter. Asaph did not regard Assur in that way by saying that "Assur *also* is joined with them." He had foreseen that Assur in the End time would be a powerful leader of the mighty Empire whose influence and dominion would dramatically change the world in the same way as the Assyrian Empire dominated the ancient world. What Psalm 83 says is that Edom (Turkey)

71

is a different entity than Assur-Germany; thought in this planned attack it appears as an ally pursuing the common goal of attacking Israel.

This kind of military alliance between Edom (the Ottoman Empire) and Germany (Assur, the former Assyrian Empire) has a long history. In 1790 the Turkish Empire signed a treaty of peace and friendship with the Kingdom of Prussia. On August 2, 1914, just shortly following the outbreak of World War I, an alliance was formed between the German and the Ottoman Empires. This German-Ottoman alliance was created to strengthen and modernize the ailing Ottoman military, as well as to provide Germany safe passage into neighboring British colonies. During WWI and WWII both countries closely cooperated as military allies and economic partners. On June 18, 1941, Turkey and Germany signed a non-aggression pact that lasted until August 1944; then Turkey severed its diplomatic and commercial relations with Germany. This alliance can be explained not only as strategically-motivated friendly cooperation, but also as a common sense of belonging to the same blood-related families of Edomites and Hittites. Their relationship has become closer over the decades. The Edomites heavily intermarried with Hittites and have become related people. Through Esau's Hittite wives (Genesis 26:34), the Hittite people were instrumental in the settlement of the Edomites in Turkey, the former Anatolia, where they had an Empire that lasted almost a thousand years. In short, the ancient Assyrian Empire possessed a large chunk of the present-day territory of Turkey and intermarried on a large scale—and because of this, there is a special, almost mystical, age-old bond between Turkey and Germany expressed in the warm, almost familial relationship between them. We are not rejecting the possibility that there are some genealogical traces of Edom among the German ruling military elite and aristocracy, but on the whole Germany consists of and represents the descendants of the Assyrian and Hittite people, the earliest civilizations in the Middle East. The presence of a Hittite blood line in both nations is essential to forming their common cultures, traditions, militarism, love of war, feelings of superiority, and quest to dominate other nations. Germany promotes and absorbs vast numbers of the Turkish Diaspora, which has become, at roughly three million people, the largest ethnic Muslim minority. Four million German tourists visit Turkey each year.

These ancient enemies of Israel, Esau and Assur, were defeated in the two World Wars by the allied forces of Israel (Joseph): Great Britain, the USA, Canada, Australia, New Zealand and others countries of Israelite origin. This trend will be repeated in the time of the fulfillment of the prophecies recorded in Psalm 83. The forces of Edom-Turkey will again form a military alliance with the forces of Assur-Germany to attack Israel on behalf of the children of Lot (Psalm 83:8). This attack will happen after Assur-Germany, which is the king of the north, defeats the king of the south (Iran) and takes full control of the Middle East (Daniel 11:40-43). Who are the allies of Germany in this war? As it was in WWII, most of the Muslim and Arab world will be allied with Germany. An ineradicable hatred of Jews is the common denominator uniting them. It will be the ten kings of the EU, Edom-Turkey, together with the countries listed in Psalm 83. On the side of the king of the south, which is Iran, will be Iraq, Syria, Egypt, Lybia, and Ethiopia (Daniel 40:41-43). The prophecy specifically mentions that the king of the north, whom we identified as Assur-Germany, will spare Edom, Moab, and Ammon, the nations that will later become the closest allies in the attack against Israel (Psalm 83). Moab and Ammon (Jordan) – the proxies of Germany – will provoke this war with Israel, as in the past (1 Chronicles, 19:1-4), and the powerful European Empire of Assur-Germany will come "to help the children of Lot."

Edom-Turkey has endured dramatic political and religious changes in recent years, but its revolution is a quiet one initiated from the top. It was the Government of the Islamist Prime Minister Erdogan and his Justice and Development Party (AKP) that transformed this secular pro-western republic envisioned by its founder Kemal Ataturk into the Muslim Republic of Turkey. It has severely disrupted its previously friendly relationship with Israel, the USA, NATO and the West. It has become the best of friends with Iran, Syria, and Lebanon and has supported all the terrorist organizations in the Middle East that fight against Israel. From the most reliable ally of Israel in the Middle East Turkey has become the most antagonistic and is now a sworn enemy of the Jewish people and their state. This openly confrontational approach to Israel and the West has boosted its prestige in the Arab-Muslim world that looks at Turkey as the regional power broker.

Only the Bible can explain Turkey's unexpected and sudden transformation. According to the Bible, these contemporary conditions will end, and Turkey will soon become the closest ally of Germany, NATO, and the EU once more, and join their common effort to fight against the king of the south (Iran) and Israel. Turkey considers EU membership an important state policy and a strategic target for the future. The outbreak of civil war in Syria was the turning point in Turkey's relationship with the Assad government and Iran. As the prophecies indicate, Edom-Turkey will not remain allied with the Muslim countries but move into the Euro-NATO camp and together with the Assur-Germany-led EU take an active role in the war of Psalm 83. Biblical prophecy confirms that this strategic partnership will be crucial for Europe to secure control of the Middle East, literally using the territory of Turkey as the land bridge for their attack against the king of the south and its allies. Edom-Turkey's future is doomed by the Almighty. What we have learned from the prophecies is that this nation will be destroyed at the hands of the Israelites for its evil sins, hatred of God and His people Israel and refusal to repent (Ezekiel 25:14).

CHAPTER IX

THE HAGARENES

There is uncertainty among scholars as to whether the names "Hagrite," "Hagarite," or "Hagarene" (Psalms 83:6) are applicable to Egypt. The uncertainty derives from accounts of the Egyptian woman Hagar (the mother of Ishmael), as well as from stories of a nomadic Arab people dwelling in Palestine, east of Gilead. Biblical sources tell us that they were defeated in the time of King Saul by "the sons of Reuben and the Gadites and half the tribe of Manasseh" (I Chronicles 5:10, 18-19). The Hagarite princes – Jetur, Nephish, and Nodab – are the sons of Ishmael as recorded in Genesis (25:15).

Others think, based on the Assyrian inscription of Tilgath-pilneser III that the Hagrites are of Aramaean origin and must be sought among the Syrian people. The author David Dolan totally excludes Egypt from a host of regional Arab powers that will attempt to destroy Israel in the prophesied end days, which means that Egypt will not participate in the confederation of the nations listed in Psalm 83. It also means that the present-day peace and cooperation between Israel and Egypt will continue throughout the coming war. Later on, when we come to the wars of the king of the south and the king of the north (Daniel 12:40-43), we will understand why Egypt is not mentioned among the plotters.

Bill Salus, supported by Dr. Arnold Fruchtenbaum, insists that the Hagarenes represent Egypt, citing Hagar's incivility toward Sarah and her status as an Egyptian. "Considering Hagar was an Egyptian according to Genesis (16:1) and had her son Ishmael marry an Egyptian bride in Genesis (21:21), we can safely conclude the Hagarenes represent Egypt in Psalm 83 through her and Ishmael's family tree," says Salus. But this identification is as wrong as the previous ones were concerning Edom and Assur. As Joel Richardson rightly notes, Hagar as an Egyptian woman, is not "the matriarch of the Egyptians." Egyptian descent does not entitle her to the status of matriarch of the Egyptian people. Egypt had been in existence long before she was born. Richardson concludes that, "Such reverse genetic engineering may make for interesting science fiction, but it is not proper hermeneutics by any stretch of the imagination." Indeed, if one uses only bloodline as the principal method of identifying the nations of old, one should widen the scope of Ishmael's influence beyond the Arabs of Saudi Arabia to a variety of countries in the Middle East and northern Africa, where his descendants dwell.

Other scholars have suggested that Hagar later remarried and had children, who became known as the Hagarenes or Hagarites. Apparently, they may have moved from this location to present day Iraq because they are mentioned later in the Assyrian records. Richardson thinks that the Hagarenes are not the Egyptians, but rather northern Jordanians. Again, he does not specify what nation or entity the Hagrites represent today. Some archeologists have speculated that the east Arabian kingdom of the Gerrhaeans may be attributed to the descendants of Hagar. If this conjecture is factual, then history tells us much more of the Hagarites, who would have been known as the Gerrhaeans in the Greek world. According to the Nabataean History blog, one of the earliest allusions to these people is found in a poem written in the third century BCE by Nicander of Colophon. There is little subsequent mention of nomadic Gerrhaeans in Chaldaean and Assyrian records. Some years later, during the time that Strabo wrote his history, the Gerrhaeans earned fame as merchants of incense. Strabo tells us that "from their trafficking both the Sabaeans and the Gerrhaeans have become richest of all [the Arabians]" (16.4.19). Strabo also recorded that, "The Gerrhaeans import most of their cargo on rafts to Babylonia and thence sail up the Euphrates with them, and then convey them by land to all parts of the country."

Analysis of Psalm 83 shows that the Ishmaelites appear to be separate from the Hagarenes and comprise two distinct groups of nations. The Ishmaelites are the descendants of Ishmael and the Hagarites are descendants of Hagar. One can find the same distinction in I Chronicles 5:19: "They waged war against the Hagrites, Jetur, Naphish and Nodab," where the sons of Hagar allied with the sons of Ishmael in the war against the Israelites. Jetur, Naphish and Nodab were the sons of Ishmael (I Chronicles 1:31). This passage could be understood differently: that is, as King Saul fighting with the Hagarite tribes of Jetur, Naphish and Nodab, making them one related nation, and in this sense, the sons of Ishmael. Supporting this notion is the fact that Muslim scholars and historians have no record of any of Hagar's descendants. This is not surprising because in the male-dominated culture of the Middle East, it is doubtful that a tribe would name itself after a female descendant. However, we need to use the prophecy of Psalm 83 as our guide; in it Asaph listed two separate groups of people: the Ishmaelite nation and the Hagarene nation. We even find Biblical evidence in the Scriptural passages, where it is said that King David appointed Obil the Ishmaelite to care for the camels and Jaziz the Hagrite to care for the flocks (1 Chronicles 27:30-31). On the basis of these passages, we may conclude that the Hagrites and Ishmaelites belong to different Arab tribes. The Bible says that the Hagarites dwelled in the desert east of the land of Israel, over towards Babylon. The Hagarites are no longer mentioned as a distinct people after the reign of King David.

Egypt will certainly not be able to take part in this confederation against Israel because in the preceding Psalm 83 war it will be captured by the victorious king of the north (Daniel 11:42-43). Egypt will suffer defeat as the closest ally of the king of the south (Iran). The problem with Salus' and others' interpretations of the nations involved in the plot of Psalm 83 is the fact that they have not connected the prophecies of Daniel and Asaph. They have not taken into consideration the role and place in the future eschatology of the new superpower of the Common Market of Europe under the leadership of Assur-Germany, as prophesied by the prophets of the Bible. The events of Psalm 83 could not possibly transpire without the participation of the countries of the "outer circle" such as Germany and Turkey. Yet, the fundamental mistake in interpretations of the nations involved in this plot has to do with ignorance of the other prophecies connected with Psalm 83, especially those prophecies dealing with God's punishment of the nations for "crafty counsel against His people."

We have outlined in detail the shortcomings of such interpretations elsewhere. What Psalm 83 actually tells us in its description of the nations is that this confederation of plotters will consist of certain moderate Muslim and Arab nations allied with a Germany-led EU as Assur and Turkey as Edom. By learning the details of the wars between the king of the north and the king of the south, one can clearly understand why Egypt is absent from the list of the plotters, why Edom is Turkey instead of the Palestinians and their "tents of the refugees," and why Assur is Germany but not Syria or Iraq. One can also comprehend the role of Assur-Germany and ascertain the real leader in this bloody conspiracy, as well as the nature of the provocative actions of the children of Lot – Ammon and Moab – the proxies of Germany (Daniel 11:41).

In defense of his position, Salus argues that those who omit Egypt from Psalm 83 need to explain Egypt's apparent future confrontation with Israel in Isaiah: "And the land of Judah shall be a terror unto Egypt" (19:16-18). Basically, Salus argues that someday Egypt will greatly fear Israel's retaliation for taking part in a secret confederation aimed at eradicating it as a nation. Further on, he mentions that Israel's defeat of Egypt and its allies in the wars of 1948, 1956, 1967, and 1973 have brought constant fear to the Egyptians, which caused President Anwar Sadat to make peace with Israel in 1979. Cursory acquaintance with the commentaries of the scholars on Isaiah 19 contradicts Bill Salus' opinion that Egypt will fear the land of Judah for its retaliation against Egypt's participation in the deadly coalition of Psalm 83. According to 2 Chronicles, in the days of the King Manasseh, Judea became subject to Assyria (33:11). The kings of Assyria Esarhaddon and his son Asshurbanipal often conducted their attacks on Egypt through the land of Judea, which is why Egypt was in constant fear of Judea. Some even say that Assyria forced Judea to be a part of its military expeditions against Egypt, which would have caused additional fear from the land of Judea because the Egyptians were aware of the cruelty and destructive power of the Assyrian armies. They knew how Judea fell and was overrun by Assyrian forces, how its land was wasted, its cities ruined, and its people slaughtered—this vision of the land of Judea instilled "terror unto the Egyptians." In accordance with these commentaries, other scholars have said that it was under the Assyrian kings Sennaherib and Sargon that Assyria, with the active subordinate ally of Judea, brutally attacked Egypt and brought calamity and destruction to the Egyptians—hence the land of Judah would be "a terror unto Egypt."

Yet others say that it was not fear of Judah's invasion but knowledge of dreadful punishment of the Assyrian army under Sennacherib (that is, the death of 185,000 Assyrian soldiers), whose terrible overthrow by God could be reversed upon Egypt, that caused them to shake in fear. No one commentator says that Psalm 83 gives reason for Egypt to be terrorized by the land of Judah.

Instead of tracing the Egyptian participation in Psalm 83 through the Hagrites or Hagarenes, as many Bible scholars have comfortably (and wrongly) done, it makes the most sense to connect them with the Aramaean people of Syria, as Mr. Armstrong suggests, because these ancient people dwelt in the area known as Syria today, or in Iraq as some others have suggested. These people were divided into small independent kingdoms and never had a unified nation. They intermingled with pre-Islamic Arabs (Hagrites, Nabateans) and had a mixed identity. This trend was particularly strong in the seventh century ACE after the Arab Islamic conquest, when forceful conversion to Islam and a tremendous influx of Arabic people and culture took place. The indigenous people became a minority, gradually lost their national identity and their country, and became Arabic in a cultural sense. After their defeat the Hagrites gradually intermingled with the nations of the region, became Muslims, and may well represent Syria, Iraq, or any other Arab tribes in Psalm 83.

CHAPTER X

AMALEK

The name "Amalek" requires investigation. These people were semi-nomadic tribes dwelling in the area of Negev, and Amalek was the grandson of Edom and a sub-tribe of Esau. The Amalekites were the sworn enemies of Israel and caused great sorrow in Israel over many generations. From ancient times, they were associated with the enemies of Moab, Ammon, Midianites, Philistines, and Edomites in the bloody battles against the Israelites (Judges 3:13; 6:3; 1 Chronicles 18:11). Rabbi Yosef Chaim Sonnenfeld (d.1932) said, "I have a tradition that Germany is Amalek." The first contact that the Israelites had with the Amalekites happened at a place called Rephidim near Sinai, where Amalek attacked Israel and was defeated (Exodus 17:8, 13). God promised Moses that He "will utterly put out the remembrance of Amalek from under heaven." A non-Israelite prophet Balaam, son of Beor, thus prophesied: "Amalek was the first of the nations; but his latter end shall be that he perishes forever" (Numbers 24:20). Why Amalek was "the first of the nations" is not clear. The

Amalekites were not that mighty leading people at that time, nor were they great in numbers or the oldest nation. Perhaps they were called so on account of the fact that they were the first people to attack Israel after the exodus from Egypt. The Israelites had continuously fought many battles against the Amalekites down through history and defeated them on many occasions, but never completely blotted them out, as God ordered. When they left Egypt under the leadership of Moses, God warned the ancient Israelites never to forget the attack of the Amalekites.

God said, "Remember what Amalek did to you on your journey out of Egypt, how he attacked you on the way, when you were faint and weary, and struck down all who lagged behind you; he did not fear God" (Deuteronomy 25:17-19). This aggravating attack on the Israelites by Amalek was unprovoked cruel and inhuman action. The Israelites had just come out of hard slavery under the Egyptians, their spirit was broken, they were not used to war, and their physical condition could be described as "faint and weary." Instead of humanely helping the exhausted Israelites by giving them food and water or any other necessary provisions, the Amalekites cowardly attacked the most vulnerable – the elderly, women, and children –from their rear and smote them with the sword. Moreover, Amalek showed no fear of God who was then in the pillar of cloud and fire with Israel, and who had done many great wonders in Egypt, of which Amalek surely had heard. King Saul defeated the Amalekites, captured their

King Agag, and "utterly destroyed all the people with the edge of the sword" (I Samuel 15:8). In the days of Hezekiah king of Judah, the rest of the Amalekites that escaped were annihilated, after which we hear of them no more. Despite this, their name appears one more time in the prophetic Psalm 83. It seems that the commandment to blot out Amalek has still not been fulfilled, "Therefore it shall be, when the Lord your God has given you rest from all your enemies round about, in the land which the Lord your God gives you for an inheritance to possess it, that you shall blot out the remembrance of Amalek from under heaven; you shall not forget it" (Deuteronomy 25:19).

It has been evident that the Amalekites were not completely annihilated in the times of Joshua, the Judges, David or Solomon. Because the Israelites violated the direct commandment of God, they were subjected to the harsh punishment of exile from the Promised Land that has lasted more than two thousand years. Since we identified Amalek with the modern day Palestinian-Philistines of the West Bank and Gaza (Hamas, PLO and closely associated Arab-Muslim jihadist groups), one can easily find their prototypes in the Biblical message. For example, "But if you will not drive out the inhabitants of the land from before you; then it shall come to pass, that those whom you let remain of them shall be barbs in your eyes, and thorns in your sides, and shall trouble you in the land wherein you dwell. And as I plan to do to them, so I will do to you" (Numbers 33:55-56). Maimonides expressed the hope that "the Lord will destroy the seed of Amalek entirely and will wipe him out to the last person as He promised." The Amalekites were characterized by two vices: cruelty and cowardice. The Biblical descriptions of the Amalekites show that they had a long and violent history of terrifying atrocities and aggressions against early Israel, raiding, plundering, and kidnapping them for the slave trade.

The Palestinians inherited the same qualities as they terrorize and massacre defenseless civilian populations, and in times of danger hiding behind their women and children using them as a shield to protect their own lives. The worst example of Amalek is Haman. In the time of the Persian King Ahasuerus (identical to Xerxes, 486-465 BCE), the descendant of Amalek, Haman, the son of Hammedatha the Agagite (Esther 3:1), whom the king advanced above all the princes in the kingdom, plotted to exterminate the entire Jewish population of the Empire. Thanks to Mordecai and Esther, the Jews were saved and evil Amman, the enemy of the Jews, was hanged together with his ten sons.

Salus connects Amalek to the Sinai Peninsula and thus to Egypt. Again, we cannot agree with his assumption. First of all, Amalek has nothing to do with Sinai (the territory of Egypt) because his territory was within the borders of southern Palestine (Negev). Secondly, approximately 3,000 years ago King David drove the Amalekites out of Negev into Transjordan Edomite territory at Mount Seir: "And some of them, even the sons of Simeon, five hundred men, went to

Mount Seir, having for their captains Pelatiah, and Neariah, and Rephaiah, and Uzziel, the sons of Ishi. They destroyed the remnant of the Amalekites who escaped, and have lived there to this day" (1 Chronicles 4:42-43).

There is no evidence in the Bible that the Amalekites lived in the modern-day Sinai Peninsula. Amalek is regarded as a rabid hater of the Jewish people and God; it may well represent contemporary terrorist organizations such as Hamas, Hezbollah, the PLO, the Muslim Brotherhood, Al-Qaeda and other Jihadists of all kinds, names, and colors. And because Amalek is part of Edom-Turkey and scattered all over the Middle East, it may well make sense to call the Palestinians of the West Bank and Gaza Amalekites. Our sages teach that God said to the Israelites, "If you do not remember Amalek, you will be sent back to the bondage of Egypt" (Pesikta Rabati 12). The fact that the Amalekites and Philistines are present in the plotters' coalition of Psalm 83 says that these people are still around and known under different names. They are characterized by the prophecy as irritant "barbs" in the eyes of the Israelites and "thorns" in their sides and back. These people will poison the Israelites lives and will not let them live in peace and security in their own land, as evident today by the Palestinians' bloody atrocities, intifadas, Gazan Wars, and terrorist rockets and suicide bombings. God says to the Israelites that if they do not get rid of these people, He will exile Israel again. It is on account of their wickedness that God pronounced His judgment to drive them out of the Holy

Land. The Israelites will listen to God and bring "the fist of God's judgment" against the Philistines and Amalekites and utterly destroy them (Ezekiel 25:15-17; Jeremiah 47:1, 4). Israel will never again be exiled from the Promised Land: "I will plant Israel in their own land. They will never be uprooted from the land I have given them" says the Lord (Amos 9:15).

CHAPTER XI

THE PHILISTINES

Who are the Philistines? What are their origins? Do the Palestinians of Gaza represent the ancient Philistine people who lived in Canaan more than three thousand years ago? Well, the Palestinian Arabs claim that they are direct descendants of the ancient Philistine people who lived in Canaan before the Israelites moved in. Their motives are understandable in light of the political battle for the land's rightful ownership in the peace negotiations. The majority of scholars (including B. Salus and J. Richardson) believe such claims. But what are the facts? The facts speak for themselves:

I. Those Canaanites, who are also called Phoenicians and Philistines, are not Arabs, and have nothing in common with them. The Philistines are not Semitic people. They are the descendants of Ham through his son Mizraim: "Mizraim was the father of the Ludites, Anamites, Lehabites, Naphtuhites, Pathrusites, Casluhites (from whom the Philistines came) and Caphtorites" (Genesis 10:13-14).

II. The Canaanites were invaders from the Aegean Sea, the Island of Crete, and Anatolian areas during the twelfth century BCE. The Canaanites and Israelites were the people who had dwelled in this land long before the Exodus from Egypt. If the Palestinians were these 'Sea Peoples' as they pretend to be, they might be justified in claiming the Island of Crete from the Greek authorities as their original homeland, but this is not the case: "Did I not bring Israel up from Egypt, the Philistines from Caphtor" (Amos 9:7)? 'Caphtor' denotes the ancient name of the Island Crete where the descendants of Caphtor, the son of Mizraim, were settled shortly after the Flood. They invaded Canaan, destroyed the people who lived there, the Avvites, and settled in their territory, as it says: "The Caphtorites coming out from Caphtor destroyed the Avvites and settled in their place" (Deuteronomy 2:23).

III. If the Philistines invaded Canaan from the sea circa the twelfth century BCE, and were thus called the Sea Peoples, the Ishmaelite Arabs invaded Palestine from the wilderness during the Arabs' conquest under Mohammed during the seventh century ACE. That wilderness is the Arabian Peninsula, the Arabs' homeland.

IV. The Philistines and Arabs are different peoples, with different racial origins, ancestries, cultures, languages and religions.

V. The Bible says that the Philistines, the Sea People, are extinct. They have vanished from history. Any Palestinian

Arab (Shem) link and identification with the Philistines (Ham) is false.

The Israelites and the Philistines had been living in the land of Canaan, the Promised Land, since the time of Abraham, the Patriarch of the Hebrews, and Abimelech, the king of the Philistines. There had been a Peace Treaty between them (Genesis 21:32). Later on, after the Exodus from Egypt, God used the Philistines as an instrument to punish and test His People Israel. The Philistines became brutal oppressors and mortal enemies of the Israelites. In the time of King David, the Israelites defeated the Philistines and subdued them (2 Samuel 8:1). The Kerethites and Pelethites were also Philistines who came from the ancient homeland of Crete. They were loyal to David and even served as his bodyguards.

As far as the Bible is concerned, the Philistines were later destroyed and vanished from the face of the earth, as the prophets of God had prophesied: "I will turn my hand against Ekron, till the last of the Philistines is dead" (Amos 1:8). Strong words against the Philistines were also issued by the Prophet Jeremiah: "The word of the LORD that came to Jeremiah the prophet against the Philistines, before Pharaoh smote Gaza. For the day has come to destroy *all the Philistines*. The LORD is about to destroy the Philistines, the remnant from the coasts of Caphtor" (47:1, 4). Many Bible scholars are of the opinion that the prophet speaks here of Pharaoh Necho who was defeated by the Chaldeans in the battle of Carchemish in 605 BCE. On the way back to Egypt, Necho attacked and destroyed the Philistines of Gaza. This was in the time of Josiah, the King of Judaea. The Philistine cities lost their independence to Assyria, and in the following years all revolts were crushed. The Philistines were subsequently absorbed into the Babylonian and Persian empires, and disappeared as a distinct ethnic group by the late fifth century BCE. The last time that the Philistines are mentioned in Scripture is in Zechariah 9:6: "Foreigners [a mixed race, Hebrew word 'mamzer,' possibly connoting a bastard people] will occupy the city of Ashdod. I will destroy the pride of the Philistines." Could it be that these 'foreigners' represent the modern-day Palestinians from Gaza and the West Bank who have falsified a claim to inheritance as if they were the rightful heirs of the ancient Philistines?

When the Israelites provoked God by worshipping idols and disobeying His commandments, God responded: "I will move them to jealousy with those which are not a people; I will provoke them to anger with a foolish nation" (Deuteronomy 32:21). "Those which are not a people" may be understood as a defective, inferior foolish nation, a people without God, not recognized by Him as the covenant people of Israel. These descriptions point to the Palestinians who are well qualified by their actions to be irrational and godless people. Besides, there is nothing proud and honorable to call them Philistines, whose social attitude can be described as materialistic, anti-intellectual, and narrow-minded. Those people undervalued and despised art, beauty, spirituality, and intellect. There is no reason whatsoever to classify the Palestinians of Gaza as the Philistine Hammitic people and the Palestinians of the West Bank as Edomite Semite people. Such classification of the Ishmaelites-Arabs of Palestine is incorrect and finds no support in Scripture or in history.

On the other hand, there is the possibility that insignificant numbers of Philistines and Amalekites survived God's judgments (it is hard to imagine a complete annihilation of nations) and dispersed among the surrounding Israel nations. As time passed, they gradually lost their knowledge of their racial origins, assimilated into existing societies, and became Arabs of Muslim faith. By the inscrutable ways of God, during the end of the nineteenth and the beginning of the twentieth centuries these people began their exodus from the Arab countries of their dwelling place to the territory of the ancient Canaan in order to fulfill the prophecy (Numbers 33:55-56; Amos 1:8; Jeremiah 47:1,4; Zechariah 9:6;Ezekiel 25:15-17; Psalm 83). So, the Palestinians of Gaza and the West Bank may well represent the fragmented people scattered all over the region—the descendants of the Amalekites and Philistines of Psalm 83. That is why the Bible calls them "foreigners" and the people "which are not a people" and "a foolish nation" or "evil neighbors." This is the exact reason why the Palestinians should be driven out of the land of Israel, which in the turn will end the fictitious Peace Process and heal Judah's spiritual wound forever (Hosea 5:13).

CHAPTER XII

THE WARS BETWEEN THE KING OF THE NORTH AND THE KING OF THE SOUTH

Of the wars between the king of the south and the king of the north, we learn much from the prophet Daniel. Chapter 11 of the Book of Daniel gives a detailed history of the transitions of kingdoms from the time of Darius to the time of Antiochus IV. The entire chapter is not of interest to us in this context. The scholars of the Bible have come to the general consensus that the contents of this chapter are a reflection of historical events that transpired in the past. Basically, the book documents the fulfilled prophecies of politico-military struggles between the two successors of Alexander the Great in the concerned region: the Seleucid Syria and Ptolemy Egypt.

The king of the north represents Syria and the king of the south represents Egypt (Daniel 11:1-35). Because the prophecies are amazingly accurate in their details, some critics have said that they must have been written after the events. Based on certain historical events of the past, most theologians have divided Chapter 11 thus: verses 1 to 4 depict the Persians and Greeks; verses 5 to 20 describe the details of the Seleucid-Ptolemy Wars; verses 21 to 32 portray the personality and deeds of Antiochus Epiphanes; verses 32 to 35 point to the Maccabees epoch. There are plenty of opinions on the historical personalities who stand behind the kings. Many view Antiochus Epiphanes (175-164 BCE) as the king of the north (11:21-32). Others identify him as the Roman Emperor Caesar Augustus, as Aurelian, or as Herod the Great (11:36-45).

Ewiak Ryszard hits upon the idea that Daniel's king of the north is the same personality as Ezekiel's Gog of the latter days. He interprets Gog as the Russian leader from the north who will invade Israel in the latter days, and as therefore the same king of the north prophesied by Daniel. Ryszard goes to great lengths in an attempt to prove his proposal. In Daniel 11:28, for instance, he sees many details concerning Russia: the history of Russia after WWII, the break-up of the Soviet Union, and the "return back into Russia's land." At one point he asserts that, "The same peoples such as Persia, Libyans and Ethiopians are named as components of their armies." As this statement reveals, his theory resembles a fairytale and does not withstand any serious Scriptural criticism. A simple reading of the names and numbers of the nations involved in Psalm 83:6-8 and Ezekiel 38:5-6 shows how groundless his position is. Besides, these two future wars will be different in timing and nature (the first being the war of Psalm 83, following the invasion of Gog), and different in purpose (in Psalm 83 the goal is "to cut them off from being a nation," in Ezekiel 38:12, "to take a spoil and a pray"). Even the land of Israel will be different in the time of Gog's attack: it will be larger in terms of geographical territory due to the defeat of the surrounding Israel nations and repossession of their lands. Therefore, the Israelites will "dwell safely, without walls, and having neither bars nor gates" (Ezekiel 38:11). If these conditions of Israel's peace and safety did not exist because of the war of Psalm 83, then the Gog and Magog wars would not have started. The wars and punishments of the nations in Psalm 83 were conducted by the hands of the Israelites; meanwhile, the defeat of Gog's armies will be performed by God Himself. One cannot find any similarities between these two wars to make one believe that they are identical. And, of course, there would not be the nations of Persia, Iraq, Syria, Egypt, Libya, and Ethiopia fighting against Israel in Psalm 83.

As we wrote before, the past events of the fulfilled prophecies of Daniel 11:1-35 are not of interest here, because we are not concentrating on the past facts of history, but rather on the future prophecies of Daniel which connect us to the theme of this work— Psalm 83. Is there any connection between Psalm 83 and Daniel 11:36-45? Yes, indeed, there is plenty of evidence that the prophets speak of the same Assur as the king of the north and the same nations involved. Even the timing is in close proximity, with the minor exception that the war of Daniel 11:40-43 would slightly precede the war of Psalm 83. As soon as the king of the north finishes with the king of the south and his allies, the prophecy of Psalm 83 will have not only begun but achieved fulfillment.

Before we reveal the name of this king of the north, it should be emphasized that his identity has nothing to do with the Seleucid King Antiochus Epiphanes, the Roman Emperors, King Herod the Great, or the Antichrist, as many have proposed. By the way, it surely cannot be the Antichrist because the title "king" is not appropriate for him and is never used in the Bible or anywhere else. The king of the north in Daniel 11:36-45 is entirely different than the one depicted in the previous verses of Chapter 11. The majority of Bible commentators have acknowledged as much. They think that this king must be of Western origins, the last tyrannical Gentile ruler before the coming of the Messiah. Many of those commentators point without hesitation to the newly resurrected Holy Roman Empire—the fourth beast or fourth kingdom of the prophecy (Daniel 2:40-42; 7:7, 24).

There are many things in verse 36 that do not apply to King Antiochus. This king will have an absolute and supreme power, "shall do according to his will," and "shall exalt himself and magnify himself above any god." Antiochus Epiphanes did not have the power or liberty to do whatever he wanted, because he was not the supreme god or king of the world. The Roman Emperors, their Imperial Government and the Senate were the supreme authorities and real rulers of the world. Antiochus Epiphanes was not a complete atheist either;

he worshipped and adored a pantheon of Greek gods and had the utmost respect for the chief of the pagan deities, Zeus, for whom he built an altar and erected a statue in the Jewish Temple. The scope of the descriptions about the king in Daniel 11:36 is much broader and different than those of Antiochus IV and an obvious indication that this is another king who will come in the future. Another matter worth mentioning concerns Egypt. As can be seen from Daniel 11:30, the king of the north did not conquer Egypt a second time because he was prevented from doing so by "the ships of Kittim." In contrast, the king of the north will defeat Egypt in the End Time and "shall have power over the treasures of gold and silver, and over all the precious things of Egypt" (Daniel 11:41-42).

It seems that verse 36 serves as a "time tunnel," ending the prophecies of the Seleucid and Ptolemy kingdoms and their wars of old by jumping more than two thousand years ahead to our age—exactly the time envisioned by the Prophet Daniel for the fulfillment of his prophecies: "Now I am come to make thee understand what shall befall thy people in the latter days; for the vision is yet for many days" (Daniel 10:14). The king of the north from the old times, whomever he might have portrayed, transformed into a new personality, representing the new times of the latter days and the new geopolitical reality of this world. This incarnation, as it were, did not pass round the king of the south too. Before Daniel 11:35, this king was universally acknowledged as Egypt. Not so in Daniel 11:36-45! This prophecy says that at the time of the end the king of the north will attack the king of the south "like a whirlwind," with chariots, and with horsemen, and with many ships. The king of the south is not alone in this prophecy; he has allies. What makes us think so is the words of the prophet, who in signifying the king of the north's victory over the king of the south, says: "He shall enter into the *countries*, and shall overflow and pass over." It will not be one country involved on the side of the king of the south—he will have a few countries on his side (Daniel 11:40). That this king of the south does not represent Egypt is clearly outlined by Daniel when he further tells us how the king of the north, after defeating the king of the south, will conduct his military campaign: "He shall stretch forth his hand *also* upon the countries: and the land of Egypt shall not escape" (Verse 42). We have already established that the king of the south and some of his allies in the region were attacked, defeated and captured (Verse 40).

What are those additional countries, then, that the king of the north wants to deal with? They are the military allies of the defeated king of the south located in Africa—Egypt, Libya, and Ethiopia. Yes, Egypt here is not the king of the south, but simply serves as one of his allies. These Arab-Muslim countries "shall be at his steps," meaning under the control of the king of the north as conquered vassals (Verse 43). None of these historical events, including those related to both the kings of the north and the south, correspond to descriptions of previous verses of Daniel 11, where the Seleucid (mainly Antiochus IV) and Ptolemy rulers were involved in endless family feuds and military campaigns. Since we have made a proper distinction between the "old" and "new" kings of the north and south in the Daniel prophecies, it is time to reveal the identities of these mysterious kings of the latter days.

CHAPTER XIII

THE KING OF THE NORTH

From the beginning of his prophetic book Daniel introduces this future king as the fourth kingdom of King Nebuchadnezzar's image which will be as strong as iron and subdue all things. He describes this mighty kingdom as having two feet and ten toes made partly of potter's clay and partly of iron. Because of this mixture, the kingdom will be divided, having both the strength of iron and the weakness of clay. The people of this kingdom will form multicultural and conflicting nations that will not be united: "they shall not hold one to another, even as iron is not mixed with clay" (Daniel 2:40-43). An explanation lies in the fact that among those European nations there are many people of Israelite descent—that is why the kingdom of the king of the north will be partly strong as iron and partly weak as clay; it depends on what percentage of Israel's elements are present in the particular country. Do we know the time of the appearance of this dreadful kingdom? Of course we do: "In the days of these kings [the ten toes] shall the God of heaven set up a kingdom, which shall never be destroyed"

(Verse 44). This prophecy concerns the arrival of the Messiah and his Messianic Kingdom. Another clue to the identity of the king of the north may be found in Daniel 7:7, where the prophet sees a fourth beast with ten horns, dreadful and terrible, and exceedingly strong. It was explained to Daniel that the beast he saw is the earthly kingdom, distinct from all kingdoms, which will arise in the latter days. This kingdom will devour the whole earth. The ten horns are the ten kings that will arise; and another will arise after them, which is distinct from the ten, and he will subdue three kings (Daniel 7:20-24). Then Daniel goes further and gives us a personal characteristic of this arrogant king who blasphemes the most High and speaks "great words" against Him, who persecutes the saints and wishes to establish himself higher than God and even "change times and laws" (verse 25).

Now, having gathered this information, we can compare it with Daniel 11:36-45, with the opinions of the sages and commentators, with the modern development of geopolitical events in the world, and we find that our quest for the king of the north has come to an end. The only kingdom with the two legs of Constantinople and Rome (the countries of the eastern and western EU today) and the ten toes representing ten kings consisting of disunified multicultural nations is the European Union. This is the newly resurrected Holy Roman Empire under the indisputable leadership of Germany. No one political entity could fit Daniel's vision in our time, except the Common Market of Europe, the world's biggest economic power comprising 500 million people. Admittedly, the EU is still emerging, as the prophecy envisioned it, but its full development is a matter of time. In 1957 six core states founded the European Community, but those member states increased to 28 by 2013. The prophecy says that the final number has to be rounded to ten. There are countries such as Greece and Spain that are losing their economic and political weight as original members of the EU, while newer members such as Poland and Finland are gaining in status. Among the candidates for EU membership is Turkey, which will probably be accepted in the near future, as the prophecy indicated. In Psalm 83, Edom-Turkey is the first on the list of the confederacy, the closest ally of Assur-Germany. England will likely be removed from the European Union.

The little horn — the leader of the EU — will be revealed and will subdue three kings. All of these details will unfold in time. Many scholars have speculated on the name of this personality. Among the suggested names are the king of Spain, Juan Carlos, the former Minister President of Bavaria and the unsuccessful candidate for the office of chancellor of Germany, Edmund Stoiber, and the former Defense Minister of Germany Baron Karl-Theodor zu Guttenberg, among others. Certainly the current chancellor of Germany, Angela Merkel, would not qualify for the title. Germany is still waiting for a strong leader who could lead the EU to fulfill Daniel's prophecies. This awaited leader, the eleventh horn of the beast power, is the king of the north. If readers remember, we started this work with the intention of understanding the prophecy of Psalm 83, which requires us to rightly identify each ancient nation according to the reality of our era. Since we recognize that Assur of Psalm 83:8 is modern Germany, we put forward that this Assur and the king of the north of Daniel 11:36-45 are the same personalities, representing the same political entity—the European Union. The prophets Asaph and Daniel spoke of the same events of the latter days. After dealing with the king of the south, we will conclude by finally identifying the nations involved in "crafty counsel" against Israel in Psalm 83.

CHAPTER XIV

THE KING OF THE SOUTH

The overwhelming majority of scholars have insisted that the king of the south in Daniel's prophecies is traditional Egypt. Their opinion even applies to the End days (verses 36-45). Some such scholars, feeling that post-revolution Egypt may not be fit to be the recognized leader of the Muslim-Arab countries in the Middle East and North Africa, compromise on the notion that future Egypt will somehow transform to meet the requirements of the Biblical king of the south. A few leading theologians even issue a warning to those who do not accept Egypt as the king of the south, saying that they do not have a correct understanding of whom the king of the south will be because they simply do not understand the fulfillment of vital biblical prophecies. This is pure nonsense refuted by Daniel's verses. We have already established that the beginning of Daniel 11:36 to 11:45 is a new, completely different prophecy of the latter days with the new players as the kings of the north and south, and with a new geopolitical reality in the world.

Daniel did not name the king of the south as Egypt in this latter-day prophecy. As a matter of fact, the prophet did not name any country that may have represented the king of the south. All he said was that the king of the south "pushed at him" and the king of the north responded militarily in a manner "like a whirlwind," entering the countries of the king of the south and his allies and "overflowing and passing over" (verse 40). As far as Daniel's story goes, the business with the king of the south at this point in time has ended—he was defeated together with the allies, and Scripture says no more about him until the future war of Gog and Magog. In this war he is mentioned again as Persia, and his allies as Libya and Ethiopia. The defeat at the hands of the king of the north did not completely eradicate these countries; as time passed, they recovered, regained their independence, and joined the forces of Gog to meet their final destiny—death on the Mountains of Israel at the hands of the Almighty.

Daniel did not mention the word "allies," but the essence of his narrative undoubtedly confirms that the king of the south had allies that were subdued and conquered by the king of the north: "he shall enter into *the countries*, overflow and pass over." But the king of the north has not finished his war campaign by defeating the king of the south and his friends in the Middle East region. He has other plans, which include warring with Israel, recapturing Jerusalem, and redirecting his war machine to North Africa, where the rest of the king of the south's allies threaten him. So, he moved his armies to

North Africa: "he shall stretch forth his hand also upon the countries," defeat Egypt, Libya, and Ethiopia and loot them of gold and silver and of all precious things (Verses 41-43). These verses of Daniel are clear proof that Egypt is not the king of the south but simply one of his allies.

Now the question is: who is this king of the south? The answer is—the Muslim Republic of Iran. Why Iran? What is so special about Iran that it "deserves" the title of the Biblical king of the south? Well, as the prophecy indicates, the king of the south has to be an influential leader in the Muslim world who will be able to unite and rule the countries of the Middle East and Northern Africa. The main motivation of this confederation of Muslim and Arab nations that cemented its unity is hatred of and aspiration for the annihilation of Israel and the "great Satan"—America and the West. But the ultimate goal of fundamentalist Islam is the resurrection of an imperialistic and expansionist Caliphate with jihad and Sharia law to achieve world domination with a capital in Jerusalem. If the conquered people will not submit to Islam voluntarily, then "we will bring the sword to your necks," as some interpreters of the Koran threaten (9:29). Fundamentalist Muslims know and accept only two realities—the House of Islam and the House of War. They do not know the third solution; it is either spiritual conversion to the one and only "true" religion of Allah, or conquest and physical destruction. In the words of Osama bin Laden, "I am one of the servants of Allah. We do our duty of fighting for the sake of the religion of Allah. I was ordered to fight the people until they say there is no god but Allah, and his prophet Muhammad. We love death. The U.S. loves life. That is the difference between us two."

Egypt cannot be considered to assume this role because it does not have such power and influence. That is why Daniel envisioned Egypt as a secondary ally to Iran, like Iraq, Syria, Libya or Ethiopia. Although countries such as Iraq and Syria are not mentioned in this prophecy, it makes the most sense to include them as allies of Iran because they have the closest relationship, and have to be treated as the countries that, to loosely borrow the words of the prophecy, the king of the north entered, destroyed, and overflowed (verse 40). The Iranian Revolution of 1979 transformed Iran from a secular, modernizing monarchy under Shah Mohammad Reza Pahlavi to the Islamic Republic under Ayatollah Ruhollah Khomeini. Iran has always been a Muslim country (since the conquest and Islamization in the time of Umar 637 ACE), but Khomeini established radical Islamic fundamentalism as a leading political force on the way to the new world Caliphate. If in the ninth century the Muslim population of Persia was about 40%, in the eleventh century the process of Islamization was fully completed, with 100% of the population identifying as Muslims. Although Iran was Islamicized, it was not Arabized. Iranians are ethnic Persians belonging to the Shiite branch of Islam. Its people still speak their own official Persian language (Farsi) and the indigenous population still consists of Persians. Islam in Iran is different and distinctive culturally, politically and even religiously. In terms of territory, Iran is one of the largest countries in the world (18th); its population consists of 78 million people. The Iranian contribution to Islamic civilization is of immense importance. Their post-revolution Constitution made a provision for the "guardian" of the Islamic Republic called "the Supreme Leader of Iran."

As is the case with the king of the north, the coming of the king of the south is the subject of various opinions and speculations. This mysterious leader-to-come has to unify the Muslim world and lead it to final victory over infidels — primarily Israel, USA, and Europe — in order to subjugate and rule the entire world under Allah and Sharia law. Sometimes this leader is called Imam Mahdi or the 13th Imam by Muslims, but his full name is Muhammad ibn Hasan al-Mahdi. The term "Mahdi" is a title meaning "The Guided One." He is the spiritual and political successor to the Islamic prophet Muhammad and his mission is to bring peace and justice to the world, presumably to the Muslim world, of course. The founder of Islam, the prophet Muhammad, thus characterized the upcoming leader: "The world will not come to an end until a man from my family and of my name shall be master of the world. When you see a green ensign coming from the direction of *Khorazan*, then join them, for the Imam of God will be with the standards who will be called al-Mahdi. The Mahdi will be descended from me."

Muhammad himself confirmed the leadership of the modern Islamic Republic of Iran in unifying and leading the Muslim-Arab world to establish the Caliphate Empire and conquer the infidel world because the Mahdi is supposed to be revealed in Iran, and "Khorazan" is Iran. If Sunni (orthodox) Islam, the largest branch of the Muslim religion, believes that an Islamic state should be led by a supreme religious and political leader known as a caliph who is elected by Muslims or their representatives and does not have to be the blood descendant of Muhammad, the Shia branch of Islam maintains that a caliph (successor) should be from the bloodline of Muhammad's son-in-law and cousin Ali. This is an ancient religious difference that is foundational to the conflict between Sunni and Shia Islam that has been simmering for fourteen centuries.

Some scholars have predicted that the president of Iran, Mahmoud Ahmadinejad (2005-2013), is fit to be the Mahdi because he believes that the Mahdi will be revealed in the time of bloody nuclear wars and great violence, when confusion, tyranny and fear will spread and terrorize the nations and they will long for a savior to come. He will be sent at a time of intense disputes and differences among people and of natural disasters such as tsunamis and earthquakes. Ahmadinejad would like to create destruction and chaos on the global stage in an Armageddon fashion that — he believes — will hasten the arrival of the Mahdi. That is why, under his presidency, Iran defied all international norms and regulations out of a rigid determination to build an arsenal of nuclear weapons capable of annihilating Israel and waging war against the West. Possession of nuclear weapons would boost the image and heighten the prestige of Iran in the eyes of the Muslim world, especially among the Shiites, and together with its worldwide fame as the official state-sponsor of terrorism and huge oil and gas reserves ranked second in the world, would make it the indisputable Biblical king of the south (Daniel 11:40).

CHAPTER XV

THE WAR BEGINS

Now that we have determined who the kings of the north and south are, let us return to the military actions of Daniel 11:40: "At the time of the end shall the king of the south push at him." It is hard to comprehend how many scholars cannot read the simple literal meaning of the words, "At the time of the end," which indicate that this is a new prophecy of the future that has nothing to do with Antioch- Ptolemy and their successors' battles in the second century BCE. Who will start this war? Daniel points a finger at the king of the south, saying that "he shall push at him." The word "push" may be understood as "collide," "attack," "engage in battle," "contend with" or, as one translator puts it, to "lock horns with him." In any case, the king of the south is an active initiator of this war. How will Iran and its allies push at the king of the north, which is Germany and her ten allied nations of the EU? Daniel did not give specific answers to this question. By his own admission, the prophet could not understand everything he was told, so we may apply an educated guess in interpreting the verse. Analyzing modern geopolitics in light of the prophecies may be key in solving this matter. Iran plays a significant role in international politics as a rogue state ruled by an authoritarian regime of radical Islamists who defy international rules and laws, abuse the human rights of its people, seek to proliferate weapons of mass destruction, and actively sponsor terrorism. Iran spends hundreds of millions of dollars to finance and train various terrorist organizations, including its proxies Hezbollah, the Lebanon-based Shiite Islamist militia, Hamas, the Palestinian Islamic Jihad, and many other militant groups in Central Asia, Northern Africa, and the Middle East, especially Israel.

The country's terrorist activities are well known to the world. In November 1979 it forced its way into the USA embassy in Tehran and took fifty-two American diplomats captive who were held hostage for 444 days. Following the 1979 revolution, Iran created special military units called the Islamic Revolutionary Guard Corps to protect and export the Islamic Revolution, and train terrorists all around the world. In October 1983 Hezbollah, under orders from Iran, bombed the USA Marine barracks in Beirut, killing 241 Americans and 58 French soldiers. In June 1985 TWA flight 847 was hijacked by Hezbollah and the Islamic Jihad demanding the release of 700 Shiite Muslim terrorists from Israeli prisons. In 1992 they suicide attacked and bombed an Israeli Embassy in Buenos Aires, Argentina, killing 29 civilians and injuring 242. In 1993 the World Trade Center in New York was bombed. The intention of the terrorists was to knock the North Tower into the South Tower and kill tens of thousands of civilians. While the attempt failed, it did kill six people and injured more than a thousand; in the 9/11 attack they finally succeeded in destroying the two Towers, killing almost 3000 people and causing at least $10 billion in property and infrastructure damage. In June 1996 Hezbollah detonated a huge truck-bomb in the city of Khobar, Saudi Arabia, killing 19 United States Air Force personnel and injuring 498 people of many different nationalities.

Iran has been heavily involved in undermining American and Western interests in Iraq, Syria, Afghanistan, and North Korea. In accordance with its official policy of wiping Israel from the map, the Iranian Government continuously supports all kinds of terrorism against Israel. By Iranian command Hezbollah targets Israeli tourists in Bulgaria, Cyprus, Thailand, Nigeria and other countries. Iran also sponsors assassinations of its dissidents and opposition leaders inside the country and abroad. The list of Iranian involvements in bombing, kidnapping, hijacking, and assassinating people has no end—Iranian state-sponsored terrorism has become more intensive and deadly today than ever.

Iran's ambition of producing weapons of mass destruction (WMD), including possessing nuclear bombs for the purpose of war, is also well known to the world. Despite first-hand knowledge of how devastating the effects of using WMD could be – over 100,000 Iranian troops and civilians victims were killed with chemical weapons during the Iran-Iraq war in the 1980s – and the prohibition (fatwa) by the Supreme Leader of Iran Ayatollah Khomeini against the development, production, stockpiling and use of nuclear weapons as forbidden practice under Muslim ethics and jurisprudence, the new Government of Iran has stayed its course of having and using nuclear weapons. Western political analysts do not trust Iran and fear that it could produce the weapon and knowingly provide them to terrorists groups hostile to Israel, the United States, and Europe. Radical suicidal Islamic terrorists would not hesitate to use the most powerful WMD and take with them as many millions of human beings as possible, because they do not value life but glorify death. Nuclear terrorism is the gravest danger the world faces. If Iran obtains the nuclear bomb, it would embolden its foreign policy; it would behave more aggressively and demandingly with the international community and the threat of war would increase dramatically. A nuclear-armed Iran is a mortal risk for Israel and moderate Arab states such as Saudi Arabia, UAE, Jordan, and Bahrain, and would greatly destabilize this region of the Middle East.

There are other reasons why Iran behaves so violently and provocatively that Western democracies could not stop or punish this rogue state. International power is shared among the four largest and most powerful nations (or groups of nations), who influence world affairs in many different spheres: China, the Russian Federation, the European Union, and the

United States of America. They are all permanent members of the United Nations Security Council. Behind Iran stands Russia and China who support the radical Muslim Republic in its drive for nuclear weapons, encourage its terrorist activity and traditionally supply it with high technology, sophisticated materials and advanced weaponry. Russia has protected Iran in the Security Council by declaring that its nuclear ambitions are peaceful, and has warned the West against military action, repeatedly vetoing UN resolutions against Iran. In response to the economic sanctions and threat of military action from the USA and the rest of the West, Iran has made a counter-threat, saying in the most unambiguous manner that it will block the Straits of Hormuz and cut-off Saudi oil supplies which account for forty percent of the world's oil flow. The USA Navy says that it is possible for Iran to close the Strait for a short time, but American military forces would prevail in a conflict with Iran in order to re-open the Strait at great cost to the Iranian armed forces.

Iran could utilize another method to "push" against Europe by using its natural resources of hydrocarbon fuel as a weapon to achieve its goals. As of today, Europe imports oil and gas for industry and heating mainly from Russia. The EU heavily depends on import for all fossil fuels. Demand for gas has been growing faster than oil and the use of gas is set to increase even further in the coming years. The recent revolution in the Ukraine, the overthrow of pro-Moscow president Viktor Yanukovych, who abandoned a trade deal with the European Union in favor of closer ties with Russia, the impossibility of paying for natural gas supplies, and continuous political and economic turmoil in this country made Russia think twice before it resumed pumping gas to the Ukraine without prepaying its bills. Russia has begun exploring other possibilities to supply natural gas to different countries like China, which could afford its prices and pay its bills on time. While we write this, breaking news comes from Shanghai, China, that President Putin of Russia and Chinese President Xi Jinping signed a 30-year gas supply contract worth more than $400 billion. This landmark deal, an epoch-making event, will affect prices not only in Europe but in the world gas market; add to that the pressure to find alternative sources of fuel and have an impact on international liquefied natural gas products. China is willing to pay for its natural gas supply over longer-term contracts. Gazprom has yet to build a pipeline to carry 38 billion cubic meters of gas annually to China. Deliveries are set to start in 2018 and could eventually ramp up to 60 BCM/year. To put that in perspective, 38 BCM/year equates to 3.7 billion cubic feet (BCF) per day.

Meanwhile, Russia cut off gas supply to the Ukraine after negotiations collapsed, motivating it to pay back the huge debt that has accumulated over recent years. Europe is also unhappy with the Russian service, high gas prices and uncertainty regarding its relationship with Russia, not to mention its practice of using its available gas flow for political reasons as has been demonstrated on a few occasions in the past. Iran could use this situation for its own interests and offer to supply Europe with an unlimited quantity of natural gas at cheaper prices and with more reliable services. Let us assume for a moment that the EU agrees to this proposition and makes a deal with Iran. Everybody is happy: Iran finds a huge profitable European market for the massive export of its natural gas; and Europe, after recovering significant investments for changing its gas supplier, begins enjoying good service and much better prices. As time passes, the relationship between the partners may sour for various reasons (Iranian state-sponsored radical Islamic terrorism, ambitions of accumulating nuclear weapons, aggression against the other country, international sanctions, or violation of this agreement), and Iran, in order to get what it wants, starts to use its "fuel weapon" against the EU. The Arab members of the Organization of Petroleum Exporting Countries (OPEC) imposed an embargo in 1973 against the United States, Netherlands, Portugal, and South Africa in retaliation for helping Israel and to gain leverage in the post-war peace negotiations. There are many ways to use the "fuel weapon" to achieve needed results. The most effective one is an oil/gas embargo—that is, to completely cut-off supply the way the Russians did to the Ukraine. Manipulating the volume of production so that prices fluctuate is another good method. European industry heavily depends on natural gas. It would not tolerate Iran trying to choke its economy. The reaction of Germany and its European allies (the king of the north) would be swift and decisive—they would strike against Iran (the king of the south) and its allies with all their European might, in a blitzkrieg manner and "overflow and pass over," that is, defeat and conquer, many countries (Daniel 11:40).

We can go on and on in describing the various ways that Iran will have "pushed" against the king of the north in Daniel 11:40, but it is not necessary. We have more than enough information to determine who the real king of the south in the Middle East is: Iran. As the theologian Gerald Flurry of *The Philadelphia Trumpet* rhetorically asked, "Who else could be the king of the south but Iran?" This scholar acutely understands Daniel's prophecy of upcoming war between the kings of the north and south in the Middle East and correctly connects these events with the war of Psalm 83. We were pleasantly surprised to learn of his insightful analysis and to see how it parallels our own understanding of these matters. Instead of criticizing him, as many scholars of the Bible do for various reasons, they should study and learn from this man for their own benefit.

CHAPTER XVI

THE ALLIES OF IRAN: IRAQ

The king of the south will not be alone in his "push" against the king of the north. How do we know it? From the information the Prophet Daniel provided. In a respond to the push, the king of the north will retaliate, defeat and overwhelm the king of the south and his allied countries, as illustrated in Daniel 11:40-43. For reasons unknown to us, Daniel did not name those countries involved in the first part of the military campaign. Of the final stage of these wars, which will be fought in Northern Africa, the prophet is more detailed and names particular countries that will ally with the king of the south: Egypt, Lybia, and Ethiopia (verses 42-43). So, who are those unnamed allied countries that will be defeated by the king of the north in the beginning of his attack in the Middle East?

The first will be Iraq. Iran and Iraq are two neighboring countries sharing a common border, history, religion, and ideology. Their populations largely consist of adherents to the Shia branch of Islam, in contrast to the predominantly Sunni populations of other Arab countries. There are indissoluble connections among the influential Shia clerics who frequently travel between the countries, as well as similar backgrounds and often blood relations. Iraq and Iran are also oil- producing countries whose combined output will soon approach or even surpass that of Saudi Arabia and to make them the larger OPEC producers. That will help Iran, the "big brother," control oil flow to different destinations and increase its power and ability to use hydrocarbon fuels as a weapon of war to pursue its goals. It could be one of the means to "push" against the European Union. The trade volume between the two countries is expected to reach $12 billion at the end of 2013. Iran's first Vice President Mohammed Ridha Rihaimi said that the Iraq and Iran alliance will amount to a "great international power." The USA effort in the Iraq war (2003- 2010) was a mistake and ended in failure. The total updated (2013) financial cost of this war for America was over $2 trillion; the human cost was the death of 4,487 US soldiers and the injuries of 32,226. An estimated 176,000 to 189,000 civilians were killed. The American goal in this war was to transform Iraq into a model Arab democracy and a strong ally of the USA, to boost its oil production, and to lower its world prices. "A new regime in Iraq would serve as a dramatic and inspiring example of freedom for other nations in the region," promised President George W. Bush. As soon as the last American soldier left Iraq in December 2011, the Shiite Muslim Republic of Iran took over the Shiite "Democratic"

Republic of Iraq politically and economically, nullifying the American war efforts and resulting in colossal losses, with Iran as the only beneficiary. It is of interest to note how the current American President envisioned the future of Iraq right after the USA military forces withdrew from Iraq in December 2011. "Everything that American troops have done in Iraq – all the fighting and all the dying, the bleeding and the building, and the training and the partnering – all of it has led to this moment of success. Now, Iraq is not a perfect place. It has many challenges ahead. But we're leaving behind a sovereign, stable, and self-reliant Iraq, with a representative government that was elected by its people," stated Barack Obama. By pulling out all the USA troops from "stable" and "self-reliant" Iraq, the President had his own "Mission Accomplished" moment. America's withdrawal from the Middle East has left the door open for all kind of terrorist groups to make a comeback. It gets even worse: those terrorists not only pose a threat to Iraq, but now they seek to destroy America and purge the region of Western influence. Such a situation, in fact, serves the Iranian interests that have a long history of supporting and harboring al Qaeda and other jihadist operatives. Yet American Vice President Joe Biden assured the world and Americans that the way Obama conducted war in Iraq would be the President's "greatest achievement."

Iraq is recovering from years of bloody war and destruction, and even managed to raise its production of oil to pre-war levels, but not as a democratic country and strong ally of the USA. Quite the opposite: the Government of Prime Minister Nouri al-Maliki has degenerated into an oppressive sectarian dictatorship with more secret prisons, killings and tortures than under Saddam Hussein. Iraq has simply become the Iranian puppet. Instead of being an ally to the USA, al-Maliki has built an extremely close relationship with its Shiite neighbor, and both countries are working closely together to drive oil prices as high as possible. During Saddam Hussein's brutal regime, Nouri al-Maliki, along with many other Shiite members of his government, were living in Iran and developed a friendly relationship with its ruling elite. The "big brother" appreciates loyalty and in turn helped al-Maliki achieve re-election in 2010, preventing his government from collapsing in a no-confidence vote. Al-Maliki knows that it is Tehran that has kept him in power and does everything he can to accommodate the wishes of Iran's government. He understands that the USA comes and goes, and that he cannot trust and rely on America in the long term, whereas powerful Iran is there to stay. Iraq, formerly Iran's deadliest rival, has become its strongest ally. Iraq has undermined all of America's efforts to implement economic sanctions again Iran, helping Iran to smuggle goods across shared borders. The USA policy in Syria directed the ousting of its President Baashar al-Assad. Here, too, Iraq cooperates with Iran by letting it use its airspace to ship weapons to Assad's government. Both of these countries support Syria and its President. As correctly observed by George Friedman of Stratfor, "Over time, the likelihood of Iraq needing to accommodate Iranian strategic interests is most likely. The possibility of Iraq becoming a puppet of Iran cannot be ruled out, and this has especially wide regional consequences." Another political analyst, Don Froomkin, observes that it is sad to see Maliki willingly turn Iraq into an Iranian vassal state especially since Iran was the main sponsor of extremist Shiite groups who fought the Iraqi government for years. Iran and Iraq are now on the best of terms. It did not take long for Sunni Saudi Arabia to figure out on which side Shiite Iraq under the leadership of Prime Minister Nouri al-Maliki will be: "He is an Iranian agent. He has opened the door for Iranian influence in Iraq," said the Saudi King Abdullah of al-Malaki. Here we have a Shiite Iran-Iraq-Syria axis which perfectly fits Daniel's king of the south and his allied countries in the region of the Middle East (Daniel 11:40-41).

Today, as we write, Iraq is again in a national crisis; the civil war is flaming up and the government of al-Maliki is on the brink of collapse. The Jihadist forces of various militant groups, under the umbrella of the Islamic State in Iraq and Syria (ISIS), have joined together to attack Shiite Iraq. They form a well-organized army of approximately 30,000 thousand and rapidly growing fanatical Sunni Muslims fighters from Iraq, Syria, Europe, America, Africa, Pakistan, and the "stan" countries of southern Russia. In Syria alone12,000 foreign soldiers fight on the side of the rebels. ISIS representatives are actively seeking to recruit Jihadist fighters in more than 60 Palestinian refugee camps in Gaza and across the West Bank, in Lebanon, Jordan and Syria, to enlist support, as they claim, for liberating the Palestinian people. Their current leader is Abu Bakr al-Baghdadi, also known as Abu Dua. The organization's budget is over $2 billion, most of it coming from controlling the oil-reach fields of Iraq and Syria, robbing banks, kidnapping ransoms, selling looted antiquities from historical sites and receiving huge funding from private donors in the Gulf States, especially from Saudi Arabia and Qatar, as well road tolls and taxes levied on population under ISIS control. ISIS has plenty of small arms and ammunition, and as a result of its successive offensive victories, it seized much of the weaponry left by Americans: armored Humvees, howitzers, tanks, grenade launchers, surface-to-air Stinger missiles and even helicopters. The fighters of ISIS have become famous for their utter cruelty, increasing numbers of atrocities, and public executions by decapitation and crucifixion. Their fanaticism in religious matters manifests itself in the imposition of radical Sunni Islamic laws and brutal violence directed against Shia Muslims, Christians, Yazidis, and Jews, often live-tweeted on social media. Their tactics shocked even the cruelest al-Qaeda terrorists who disavowed them as too extreme. In February 2014 al-Qaeda cut off all ties with ISIS. The goal of ISIS is to create a Sunni Islamic caliphate with strict draconian Sharia laws on the territories of Iraq, Syria, Levant or the Eastern Mediterranean including Lebanon, Cyprus, Palestine, Jordan, and southern Turkey. The group has begun imposing Sharia law in any town they capture. Under the strict Islamic Sharia doctrine, non-Muslims living under their sovereignty must pay a special tax – known as the "Jizyah" – in return for the ruler's protection. Tens of thousands of Christian families fled the territories under ISIS control after it issued an ultimatum to Iraqi Christians: convert to Islam, pay a fine, or face "death by the sword." The Patriarch Louis Sako laments: "For the first time in the history of Iraq, Mosil is now empty of Christians." ISIS robbed them of money, properties, and of all their belongings. They envision an Islamic caliphate as reminiscent of Taliban-held Afghanistan or Al Shabaab in Somalia, with summary executions for traitors, amputations for thieves, and stonings for adulterers.

In Syria ISIS faces resistance from anti-government rebels in the west. Russia, Iran and its proxy Hezbollah would effectively prevent ISIS from dismantling President Assad's regime and taking over Syria. The moderate Syrian Sunnis and Alawites would also not accept brutal ISIS rule. In Iraq it is facing massive opposition from the Shia population in the south and Kurds in the north. But the most important enemy for ISIS is the mighty Shia Iran, which values its alliance with Shia Iraq even more than with Syria. Iran will do everything possible to secure the Shia government of Prime Minister Nouri al-Maliki (or any other Shia leader loyal to the Iranian regime), and its combined forces will put an end to ISIS and liberate Iraq and Syria. Thanks to the decisive victory of the

Iranian and Iraqi armies, substantial help of the USA, and its allies' air strikes and assistance from the Kurdish peshmegra fighters, ISIS will disappear as suddenly and unexpectedly as it appeared on the international scene. Such is what Bible predicts in describing the wars between the king of the north (a Germany-led European Union) and the king of the south (Iran) with its allies of Iraq, Syria, Egypt, Libya, and Ethiopia.

CHAPTER XVII

SYRIA

Is Syria an ally of Iran too? Of course it is. The friendship began in the direct aftermath of the Iranian Revolution in 1979, when Ayatollah Khomeini decided to use Syria as a conduit to the Shiite community in Lebanon in order to increase the influence of southern Lebanon which was fighting against Israel at the time. Syria and Iran have become close strategic allies since the Iran-Iraq war, when Syria sided with non-Arab Iran against its then common enemy of Saddam Hussein's Iraq. The alliance has also conspired against the United States and Israel. It has supported all the terrorist organizations in the Middle East fighting against Israel, especially those of Hezbollah in Lebanon, Hamas in Gaza, the Muslim Brotherhood in Egypt, and the Islamic Jihad in Palestine. Syria also signed a mutual defense agreement with Egypt in November 1966.

From the beginning of the Syrian Civil War in March 2011, Iran was heavily involved in an extensive, expensive, and integrated effort to keep the regime of President Bashar al-Assad in power. Their strategic political unity was not based on religion because Syria is a secular state with a largely Sunni Arab population, and Iran is a Shiite Islamic Republic, although Assad represents the minority Alawite branch of Shia Islam. Whereas Iran strives for hegemony and indisputable military leadership among the Muslim-Arab countries in the Middle East and Africa, Syria needs Iran for political and military protection and for help in its fight against Israel. The destruction of Israel is the most cherished wish of both countries—this stimulus motivates and unites them more than anything else in the world. This cooperation was legalized on June 16, 2006, when the Defense Ministers of both countries signed an agreement for military cooperation against what they called the "common threats" presented by Israel and the United States. "Iran considers Syria's security its own security, and we consider our defense capabilities to be those of Syria," declared the Syrian Defense Minister. Syria plays an important role in directing the flow of weapons from Iran to Hezbollah, a Lebanese Shiite army of terrorists. It created this army on the northern borders of Israel and armed it with thousands of sophisticated rockets to build the strongest military force in Lebanon in the event that Israel invades Syria or attacks Iran's nuclear facilities. In the ongoing Syrian civil war Iran stands firmly behind the Assad regime, sending it weapons and ammunition, and involving its Republican Guards in training personnel and providing technical support and intelligence. Iran ordered Hezbollah, its proxy, to intervene in this war on the side of the Assad Government. The Iranian Foreign Minister, speaking of the importance of Syria, swore that, "Iran is not prepared to lose this golden counterweight to Israel."

Behind Syria, as is the case with Iran, stand the two world superpowers of Russia and China who are permanent members of the UN Security Council and have vetoed any resolution put forward by the international community, refusing to condone sanctions or provide military support for rebels. Russia is traditionally known in the Arab world as a reliable supplier of weapons and military hardware, a very profitable trade that started in the Soviet era. Syria buys a lot of Russian military exports. From 2000 to 2010 Russia sold around $1.5 billion worth of arms, making Damascus Moscow's seventh-largest client. The President of Russia, Vladimir Putin, issued a chilling warning that Russia would stand by Syria if the USA or NATO launched air strikes against the Assad regime. Syria agreed for Russia to have a Mediterranean naval base for its Black Sea Fleet located in the Syrian port of Tartus. Russia renovated and converted this facility into a permanent Middle East naval base for its nuclear-armed warships, which is very important strategically for its foreign policy. By gaining full access to a Cypriot sea port, Moscow gradually increased fleet size and stepped up patrols in the East Mediterranean. They recently announced the establishment of a Mediterranean naval task force on a permanent basis. Meanwhile, the USA naval presence in the East Mediterranean is diminishing due to the heavy consequences of wars in Iraq and Afghanistan, and Washington does not want to get dragged into additional conflict in the Middle East. Contributing to this decision are the USA new energy finds and its aspiration toward oil-gas independence, which move their priority policy making strategy in the Middle East to an interest of minor importance. Iran also values its relations with Syria as an important bargaining chip in the regional balance of power and envisions using it as a satellite in its foreign politics.

CHAPTER XVIII

EGYPT

The relationship between Egypt and Iran has a long and bumpy history. Their friendship reached new heights in 1939 when both countries upgraded diplomatic relations to the ambassadorial level. In the same year, the sister of King Farouk I, princess Fawzia of Egypt, married the crown prince Mohammad Reza Pahlavi, the future king of Iran. This union helped forge ties and narrow differences between Sunni and Shia, effectively improving relations between these great civilizations. However, with the popular revolution following the military coup d'état under the leadership of lieutenant colonel Gamal Abdel Nasser (1918-1970) and his organization of Free Officers, the monarchy was abolished and the Republic of Egypt declared on June 18, 1953. In the time of his presidency (1964-1970), Nasser has established strong relations with the Arab countries and Soviet Union, but gradually distanced Egypt from the West, Iran, and Israel. As a still-royalist country ruled by the Shah of Iran Mohammad Reza Pahlavi (1941-1979), Iran had close relations with the West, especially the USA and Israel. This situation, together with the Sunni-Shia sectarian difference, resulted in open hostility between Cairo and Tehran for many years. When President Anwar Sadat took power in 1970, he quickly turned the relationship with Iran from one of bitter enmity into open friendship. He also improved damaged relations with the West and directed Egyptian foreign policy toward normalized relations with Israel. This attitude was appreciated by the monarchy in Tehran whose foreign policy had a predominately Western orientation. The President of Egypt conquered Iranian hearts after the speech he gave in their parliament in fluent Farsi, outlining the significance and greatness of both ancient civilizations and their historic connections. This speech so impressed the Shah of Iran that he called Sadat my "dear brother."

A new downfall in relations occurred after the Iranian Islamic Revolution in 1979. The Shah of Iran was deposed and spent the last months of his life in exile in Egypt. No country, including the USA, would grant him a visa to stay. All the Shah's former friends and allies turned against him— the same way that they betrayed Saddam Hussein of Iraq, Muammar Gaddafi of Libya, and Hosni Mubarak of Egypt. Only President Sadat humanely accepted him, and when the Shah died, Sadat ordered that he be given a state funeral, which caused the great displeasure of Ayatollah Khomeini. What most soured relations and caused tension between the countries was Sadat's Camp David 1979 Peace Accord with

Israel. Iran became furious and cut off relations with Egypt and even ceased direct flights to the country, making Egypt the only Arab country without an embassy in Iran. The radical mullahs of Iran hated President Sadat so badly that after his assassination in October 1981 a street in Tehran was named after the ringleader of the assassins.

During the presidency of Hosni Mubarak (1981-2011), relations between Iran and Egypt did not much improve. The government of Egypt did not approve the Islamic Republic of Iran's support for the terrorist groups Hamas and Hezbollah. In its view these terrorist organizations are serious threats to regional peace and stability. Hamas is a violent offshoot of Egypt's Muslim Brotherhood, which assassinated President Sadat. The Muslim Brotherhood has been banned by the Egyptian government, and Iranian support for Hamas is considered interference in Egypt's internal affairs and a challenge to its national security. Mubarak also accused Iran of supporting Egyptian al Jihad and was angered over Iran's refusal to rename a Tehran street it had dedicated to Sadat's assassin. Meanwhile, Egypt has maintained close relations with the USA and Europe and kept its provisions of the peace treaty with Israel intact. In the eight year Iraq-Iran war Egypt openly took the side of Iraq. All of these actions of the Egyptian president irritated Iran and failed to normalize relations. By the year 2007 relations had begun to improve due to diplomacy and economic trade, but between 2008 and 2009 politicians of both countries began blaming each other for inaction regarding the escalation of the Israel-Gaza conflict. Egypt has not approved Iran's nuclear program and views it as a potential threat to the region. Under Hosni Mubarak Egypt distrusted Iran and enjoyed strong relations with the US and Saudi Arabia as a Sunni bulwark against the Shiite Islamic republic. Mubarak understood that acquiring Iranian nuclear weaponry would not only pose a threat to Egypt independence and survival, as well as incite war, but would also start a nuclear armament race among countries, especially among those rich Arab nations who can afford such weapons. President Mubarak was strongly aware of US foreign politics and was by no means the puppet of the Islamic Republic of Iran.

In February 2011, as the result of mass uprising, Mubarak officially resigned as the President of Egypt, and relations with Iran rapidly started to improve. For the first time since 1979, Iran was allowed by Egypt to use the Suez Canal to let through two warships for exercise training. In April 2012, Iran sent an ambassador to Cairo. Islamist Ayatollahs were more than happy to see the election of President Mohamed Morsi (30 June 2012 to 3July 2013), who was a representative of the Egyptian Muslim Brotherhood Party. Morsi did not even try to hide his intention to recreate an Islamic Caliphate. He pardoned and freed hard-line Islamists – including Anwar Sadat's assassins – and allowed them to have an Islamic political party. He released members of Gama'a al-Islamiyya, founded by the "Blind Sheikh," Omar Abdel-Rahman, who attempted to destroy the World Trade Center. The United States considers these groups terrorist organizations. In August 2012, Morsi visited Iran and bilateral diplomatic relations were reestablished. The Egyptian government's spokesperson said: "The former regime used to see Iran as an enemy, but we do not." Both countries exchanged visits of high-ranking officials. President Ahmadinejad assured the Egyptians, "Egypt is cherished and we will invest with all our weight, we are more than ready to put our expertise and capabilities at Egypt's service. Egypt's prosperity is prosperity for Iran, and vice versa." A 2012 poll conducted by the Israel project shows that 61% of Egyptians are supportive of Iranian nuclear development. In the same year, the Egyptian parliament passed a resolution that declared that, "Egypt will never be the friend, partner or ally of the Zionist entity (Israel), which we consider as the first enemy of Egypt and the Arab nation."

After winning the first round of Egyptian elections, the Muslim Brotherhood raised the possibility of closer relations with the Islamic Republic of Iran and breaking the Peace Treaty with Israel. During his tenure, Morsi strengthened ties with Iran following several pre-revolutionary years of animosity between the two countries. The Iranian President, Mahmoud Ahmadinejad, visited Egypt in February 2013, making him the first Iranian president to travel to Egypt since the Islamic Revolution. In the short period since he has been in power (in a little under two years), Morsi has sought to turn Egypt into an Islamic religious state by imposing the

Brotherhood's views of Islam. By focusing exclusively on this issue, he has mismanaged the economy, restricted religious freedoms and done nothing to improve the everyday living conditions of the Egyptian people that led to the second mass Revolution.

On 3 July 2013, Mohamed Morsi was removed from the presidency in a military coup d'état by Field Marshal Abdel Fattah el-Sisi. The head of the Supreme Constitutional Court, Adly Mahmoud Mansour, was appointed as the new interim president. The Constitution was suspended and parliament was dissolved according to the demands of massive Egyptian protests against the first democratically elected head of state in Egyptian history. The Mansour government cracked down on Morsi followers and arrested more than 2000 Brotherhood members, including Mohamed Badie, the party's leader. More than 1000 people were killed in a week of violence between Morsi supporters and security forces after police dispersed their protest camps in a deadly operation.

When Morsi, one of the leading figures of the Brotherhood, won the presidential elections in June 2012, Iran rushed to congratulate him and called his victory one of the 'final stages of the Islamic Awakening.' Surprisingly, the US government has also supported the Muslim Brotherhood since President Obama made his "New Beginning" speech at al-Azhar University in Cairo in June 2009 and openly backed President Morsi's regime. One Egyptian commented on the US position thus: "OK, you did something good when you killed Osama bin Laden, but now Americans are with the Muslim Brotherhood, who are not much different from Al Qaeda. You support the terrorists. Why are you siding with the forces of oppression and assisting them to transform Egypt to become another Syria, Somalia or Afghanistan?" The Obama administration was greatly disappointed when the second – corrective – revolution resulted in the deposal and arrest of President Morsi and the persecution of aggressive members of his Muslim Brotherhood party. It was on the verge of cutting off 1.3 billion in annual funds to the Egyptian military.

In the opinion of the former Israeli ambassador to Egypt Zvi Mazel, it was clear to any objective observer that Morsi's goal was to establish a new Islamic dictatorship by monopolizing legislative and judicial powers and stuffing all the government ministries with Muslim Brothers. The position of the USA is hard to understand because the new interim regime of Mansour and el-Sisi is fighting against the Muslim Brothers and radical Islam in general, and is therefore acting in the best interests of the United States. The Muslim Brotherhood International organization was founded in Egypt in 1928 with the purpose of establishing a worldwide Islamic state. Their motto is: "Allah is our objective. The Prophet is our leader. The Quran is our law. Jihad is our way. Dying in the way of Allah is our highest hope." In the memo, Brotherhood leaders indicate that they plan to create an Islamist state in the United States, "destroying the Western civilization from within and 'sabotaging' its miserable house by their hands and the hands of the believers so that it is eliminated and God's religion is made victorious over all other religions." This terrorist organization has openly declared jihad against the West and Israel, killed innocent civilians, demolished ancient monuments and historic churches and synagogues, set hospitals on fire, murdered Christians in the streets, and shown the utmost disrespect for the rule of law. According to Mazel, American policy toward Egypt is part of larger policy failings in the Middle East. "With very complicated and twisted policies by the United States toward Iraq, and then what happened in Libya, Syria, and now Iran, many simply do not believe that American policy in the region is rational or reasonable. For us in Israel, it is very difficult to understand the recent American position toward Egypt," he said.

On June 8, 2014, Field Marshal Abdel Fattah Sisi, 59, officially announced the President of the Arab Republic of Egypt. Under the Constitution of Egypt, the President is the head of state and the supreme commander of the armed forces and the head of the executive branch of the Egyptian government. He received the majority of the casted votes (about 92.9%) and won the election. At the swearing-in, the Supreme Constitutional Court deputy head, Maher Sami, said ousting of the former President Morsi was not a coup, and that Mr. Sisi had responded to the will of the people. In his inauguration speech in front of foreign heads of state and international dignitaries he said that there would be no reconciliation with anyone who had blood on their hands. "Defeating terrorism and achieving security is the top priority in the coming phase. There will be no acquiescence or laxity shown to those who resorted to violence," warned the President. While Egypt was under the rule of the provisional government, the interim President Adly Mansour reinstated previously discontinued direct flights between Cairo and Tehran on March 2013 and positively re-evaluated tourism programs with Iran. The Ministry of Foreign Affairs stated that Egypt seeks stable and positive ties with the Islamic Republic of Iran. The position of the new president towards Iran has not been announced yet. If he truly views the Iranian Ayatollah's regime as an opponent, he will not go alone with Iran to support Syrian Bashar al-Assad's government; he will certainly support the Syrian Revolution and stand by its forces. By implementing foreign policies independent of Iran, Egypt would strengthen its ties with Saudi Arabia, the United Arab Emirates, Jordan and the rest of the moderate Arab states. However, there are diplomatic sources saying that Cairo tried its best to explain to the Iranians that the Muslim Brotherhood is in the past, and that the new leaders of Egypt today are interested in real and solid relations with Iran. Egypt's new foreign minister, Nabil Elaraby, said that Cairo did not consider Tehran an enemy and would turn a new page with all countries, including Iran.

Nevertheless, the Bible verses say that in the latter times Egypt will fall under Iranian influence and become the ally of the king of the south, which is Iran. Is this scenario possible?

Of course, especially when the Bible says so! The situation in Egypt could change any moment, if this president or the next one fails to deliver what the Egyptian masses expect. The Muslim Brotherhood, with the enthusiastic help of the radical Islamists of Iran, could return to power stronger and more determined than before. Let us not forget that Egypt is an Islamic country comprising eighty million Muslims that are 95% of the entire Muslim population. Although the majority of Egypt's Muslims are Sunni, Islam has been recognized as the state religion, and it is easier for Iran with its Islamic radical ideology of jihad and the world Caliphate to bring the Egyptian Muslims under the Iranian sphere of influence through the leadership of the Muslim Brothers. This will be bad news for Israel and the West. Unfortunately, something like this will happen in order to fulfill the prophecy. We have to disappoint those scholars who have insisted that Egypt is the traditional king of the south of Daniel 11:40. This is not the case. The simple literal meaning of the words of the Prophet Daniel totally excludes this possibility, making Iran the king of the south and Egypt his ally.

CHAPTER XIX

LIBYA

Libya is also mentioned in Daniel's prophecy describing the military campaign of the king of the north (Assur-Germany) against the three allies of the king of the south (Iran) from Northern Africa. If you recall, these allies are Egypt, Libya, and Ethiopia (Daniel 11:43). Libya is the one of the oldest nations on earth. Its indigenous peoples are a rich mixture of ethnic groups, primarily Berber tribes that occupied the area for thousands of years before the beginning of human records in ancient Egypt. During its long history Libya has witnessed the domination of the many civilizations and empires that have ruled its land: Carthage, Phoenicia, ancient Greece, Persia (modern Iran), Rome, the Byzantine Empire, the Islamic Caliphate, Ottoman Turkey, and Italy.

After defeating the Ottomans in the Italo-Turkish War of 1911-1912, Italy formed the so-called Italian Libya colonies of Cyrenaica and Tripolitana. The Italian governor Marshal of the Air Force Italo Balbo, who was named "the Father of modern Libya," promoted and organized the creation of the Libyan state and initiated the integration of Italian immigrants with the Arab population. Some 150,000 Italians settled in Libya, which consists of roughly 6.5 million people today. As a result of the Arab conquest in the seventh century ACE, the majority of Libya's inhabitants are the Arabized Berbers whose religion is Islam. After WWII, from 1943 to 1951, when Italy relinquished all claims to Libya, Tripolitana and Cyrenaica came under British administration, while the French controlled Fezzan. On November 21, 1949, the UN General Assembly issued a resolution stating that Libya should become independent before January1, 1952. The modern history of independent Libya began in 1951. In December 1951, Libya became known as the United Kingdom of Libya, a constitutional and hereditary monarchy under King Idris, Libya's only monarch. Some historians compare King Idris to Mahatma Gandhi and Nelson Mandela for his principle of peaceful co-existence and non-interventionist philosophy. During his rule, the discovery of significant oil reserves in 1959 and the subsequent income from petroleum sales enabled one of the poorest nations to establish an extremely wealthy state. On September 1,1969, while King Idris was in Turkey for medical treatment, a small group of military officers led by the 27 year-old army officer Muammar Gaddafi staged a bloodless coup d'état and deposed the King. It was the beginning of the Libyan Revolution. Colonel Gaddafi seized power and ruled the Libyan Arab Republic for 42 years

(1969 to 2011), and then was ousted and killed in the Libyan civil war.

The political relationship between Libya and Iran began in 1967, when both countries were governed by monarchies: King Idris in Libya (1951-1969) and Shah Mohammad Reza Pahlavi (1941-1979) in Iran. The friendship did not last long. As a result of the Gaddafi revolution, the monarchy was abolished and the Libyan Arab Republic proclaimed. Gaddafi joined the Arab leaders' alliance with Gamal Abdel Nasser, Yassir Arafat and Hafez al-Assad against the Shah of Iran, the last pro-Western king who was accused of betraying Arab interests and supporting Israel. During the national Islamic Revolution in 1979, the Shah was overthrown and died in exile in Cairo, Egypt on July 1980. After this, relations between Iran and Libya significantly improved. When the Iran-Iraq war broke out, Libya together with Syria, China and North Korea took the side of Iran and provided crucial military assistance by sending weapons, particularly missiles, to Iran. The Libyan military consultants also assisted the Iranians in their war against Iraq. Gaddafi was the key Iranian ally in this war. He sent messages to all the Arab leaders "to stand on the side of the Islamic brothers in Iran." The United States characterized the ties between Libya and Iran as "a broad relationship" and believes that military arms, including the sophisticated naval mines used by Iran in the Gulf Sea, were smuggled from Russia through Libya. In connection to this, in September 1987 the US Department of State sent a threatening note to the Libyan government, warning it against delivering Russian navy mines to Iran because the mines were hindering navigation in the Gulf Sea. Washington warned Libya against exchanging advanced navy mines for Iranian chemical weapons. On the side of Iraq were the Gulf States, Saudi Arabia, the USA, France and the Soviet Union. The Iraqi government was so upset with Gaddafi participation in the war on the side of Iran that on June 27, 1985 Baghdad broke diplomatic relations with Libya and announced its withdrawal as a member of the Arab League.

The Iran-Iraq war (1979-1988) was one of the most strategically important conflicts of modern times because it involved two major oil producers in the region where more than half of the world's reserves are located. It was also a war motivated by religion where Muslims fought against Muslims. For Ayatollah Khomeini, the regime of Saddam Hussein of Iraq was anti-Islamic, which is why he wanted to overthrow it. The alliance between Libya and Iran after the war has continued to be comprehensive and friendly. In Iran's presidential election of 2009, when Mahmoud Ahmadinejad became President of the Islamic Republic, Gaddafi was one of the first Arab leaders to congratulate him and express wishes of progress and success for Iran. High-ranking officials from both countries have regularly visited Tripoli and Baghdad and have extended bilateral ties in economic and military relations. In January 2010, the visiting Foreign Minister of Iran discussed with his counterpart in Tripoli the prospect of jointly developing oil and gas projects and building infrastructure like factories, roads, and hospitals—a new level of Iranian-Libyan cooperation. Former Iranian president Hashemi Rafsanjani and Supreme Leader Ali Khamenei were among two high-profile leaders to visit Libya when Muammar Gaddafi was at the height of his power. At the UN Security Council Gaddafi instructed the representatives of Libya to defend Iran's nuclear program and vote against binding international resolutions to enforce sanctions against the Muslim Republic.

In 2011 Libya experienced a full-scale revolt against Gaddafi and his government, which catapulted the country into civil war between forces loyal to Colonel Gaddafi and those seeking to oust his regime. The forces opposing the Gaddafi government won the war and established an interim governing body, the National Transitional Council (NTC). In September 2011, the National Transitional Council was recognized by the United Nations as the legitimate representative of Libya, replacing the Gaddafi government. On October 20, 2011, Gaddafi was captured near Sirte, the city of his birth, and killed. The National Transitional Council declared the liberation of Libya and the official end of the war on October 23, 2011. Iran reacted very quickly to the rapid changes in Libya without Colonel Gaddafi and readjusted its policy towards the new provisional government by extending its congratulations and acknowledging it as a legitimate representative body of the Libyan people. The

Iranian news agency said that Gaddafi's death meant "the end of history's despots and oppressors" and described his regime – despite the fact that it had been Iran's key ally only a few months before – as "the black dictatorship." Tehran views the Libyan revolutionaries as part of a region-wide "Islamic awakening." The Iranian government expressed the country's willingness to transfer its expertise to Libya and participate in the reconstruction of the country. Ayatollah Ali Khamenei condemned NATO and the USA for their military intervention, charging that the Western allies carried out an armed operation not for humanitarian reasons related to defending the people of Libya, but for economic reasons related to interest in Libyan oil and the desire to pursue a new form of colonialism. The Iranian ministry of foreign affairs issued a similar statement which echoed the Supreme Leader: "These countries enter usually with seductive slogans of supporting the people but they follow their own interests in ruling the countries and continuing colonialism in a new form."

Libyan-Iranian relations will further strengthen and consolidate with time, and Libya, as well as many other Islamic countries-allies, will be under the influence of the radical Ayatollah regime in their joint efforts to establish an Islamic Caliphate with Sharia laws in order to rule the world "from sea to sea." What makes us sure of this conclusion? Not only the word of God (Daniel 11:40-43), but also the current political, religious, and economic situation in Libya. As a result of the civil war, at least 30,000 Libyans were killed and 50,000 were wounded, of which about 20,000 were serious injuries. In mid-2013 the country plunged into political and economic crisis. Libya has almost entirely stopped producing oil and the central government has lost control of much of the country to militia fighters. The state's territory has become divided and is controlled by hundreds of militia, which now pose the most formidable threat to the political process. These "liberators" of Libya refuse to disarm and openly challenge the transitional authorities. Some oil-rich regional politicians call for political autonomy or self-rule and intend to keep the oil profits for themselves rather than send them to Tripoli. Various rival militia groups and its commanders fight each other, regularly harass government officials, and are unaccountable to any authority. Post-civil war chaos has become an everyday lived reality. The national army and security forces are not well organized, trained, or disciplined. It will take time to make them strong and efficient. Of the Arab-Berber population of Libya, almost all are Sunni Muslims. The Al-Qaeda terrorist organization and revived local and international Jihadists groups that are taking advantage of the new environment and actively operating in Libya constitute a significant threat to the state-building process. They are using Libyan territory as a safe haven and staging ground for their attacks. Gaddafi's vast stores of weapons, including surface-to-air missiles, plus $500 million worth of weapons intended for Libyan rebel fighters, have flowed freely into neighboring countries, thanks to porous and insecure borders, and replenished the armament of the numerous militias. The Libyan rebels have refused to give up arms, and bloody clashes between tribes have thrust the fragile nation into anarchy. The 2014 UN report revealed that "most arsenals continue to be controlled by non-state armed groups and governing institutions have very limited capacity to control Libya's borders, sea ports and airports, which contribute to the overall insecurity in the surrounding region and within Libya." Iran is well known for its support of state terrorism in the Middle East and around the world, especially of those terrorist groups and organizations that fight against Israel and the West. The radical Muslim Republic of Iran will take advantage of this chaotic situation in Libya and use all of its military and ideological power to bring this country into its sphere of influence, thus fulfilling the prophecy of Psalm 83.

CHAPTER XX

ETHIOPIA

It is not clear yet how and when the Federal Democratic Republic of Ethiopia, which has been a monarchy for most of its history, will become an ally of radical Islamic Iran. Ethiopia was one of the first countries in the world to officially accept Christianity, which has been the faith of the majority of the population since the fourth century ACE, with Christians making up 62.8% of the country's population of 94 million. Muslims, mostly Sunnis, constitute about a third of the population.

During the reign of Haile Selassie, the Emperor of Ethiopia (1930-1974) – who claimed his origin from King Solomon and Queen Sheba and often legitimated his dynasty by calling it the "Conquering Lion of Judea" – the relationship between Israel and Ethiopia was friendly. In December 1960, when Emperor Haile Selassie I was on a state visit in Brazil, some high-ranking officers of the Ethiopian army attempted a coup, but the rebellion was crushed with the help of an Israeli intervention. This warm relationship was broken in

October 1973 as a result of pressure by Arab states that sought to isolate Israel after its great victories in the 1967 and 1973 wars. Although Addis Ababa claimed that it had terminated its relationship with Israel, military cooperation between the countries continued. In 1983, for example, Israel provided communications training, and in 1984 Israeli advisers trained the Presidential Guard and Israeli technical personnel served the police. In exchange for Israel military assistance to Ethiopia, the Mengistu government cooperated in Operation Moses in 1984, in which 10,000 Ethiopian Jews (Beta Israel) were evacuated to Israel. Both countries re-established diplomatic relations in 1992. Ethiopia has an embassy in Tel Aviv and Israel has an embassy in Addis Ababa. In 2012, an Ethiopian-born Israeli, Belaynesh Zevadia, was appointed Israeli ambassador to Ethiopia.

In attempting to spread its influence on the African continent, Iran has focused on strengthening its military and economic ties with the government of Ethiopia. Both countries are cooperating well, steadily increasing their annual investments in trade, including oil, agriculture and natural resources. As a member of the Non-Aligned Movement, Ethiopia welcomes the cooperation extended by the Islamic Republic of Iran and has reaffirmed that states' choices and decisions regarding peaceful uses of nuclear technology and fuel cycle policies must be respected. This statement clearly shows Iran's influence and the support of Ethiopian foreign policy for approving Iran's nuclear ambitions. Iran's ambassador to Ethiopia has assured Iran's readiness to commit to further investment in the African country in the areas of energy, power transmission, and the construction of railroads and housing. "We acknowledge that Ethiopia has achieved a lot during the last decade and our country is ready to support Ethiopia to continue these processes. We are the symbols of the oldest civilizations; thus, we need to strengthen our bilateral cooperation," said the ambassador on behalf of the Islamic Republic. Iran is also looking forward to having continued political consultations and dialogue with Ethiopia in order to share ideas and coordinate policies while engaging in different international and regional issues.

Recent events in Saudi Arabia, from where more than 115,000 Ethiopian workers were forcefully deported under brutal conditions, have made a poor impression on the Ethiopian Government and its people. There is ever-growing Ethiopian resentment toward Sunni Arabs. The Saudi Government and its population does not distinguish between Christian and Muslim Ethiopians; its fury was directed at Ethiopians in general. The attitude towards Iran is a little bit different because Iranians are Persians, not Arabs, and do not speak their language. Generally, but with some exceptions, there is a positive perspective among people on the Ethiopia-Iran relationship. "If Iran comes with oil money they want to spend, then we open our doors, but if they come with 'Satanic Versace Bags' full of jihadist propaganda and religious Islamic fanaticism, then we close the door in their hairy mullah face," says one respondent. Another one advises the Ethiopian Government to avoid the Iranian Mullah terror at all costs, because "Ayatollahs and Shiite predicators will force Ethiopians to speak the Farsi language, study Iranian culture, and convert to Shia Islam. All the countries colonized by Muslim Arabs become zombies. They lose and abandon their original pre-Islamic identity and instead glorify their newly acquired Bedouin Arab culture. This is also true of Iran. Beautiful Persian philosophy, poetry, music, art and religion are out. If Iran wants to build places of worship in Ethiopia, let us first see a Christian Church constructed in Mecca, then we talk about your constructions in my country," comments another Ethiopian patriot ironically.

Yet, many Ethiopians stand for a closer relationship with Iran and characterize the Muslim Republic in a much friendlier way, saying that Iranians are not the Western media erroneously portrays them, but among the most friendly, wise, proud, innocent, generous, hard-working and civilized people. That is why a great and ancient nation like China has the closest relationship with Iran. Ethiopia must also have good relations with Iran as both nations benefit in the short – as well as the long – term.

Most likely, Ethiopia will follow the pattern of its neighbors' 'revolutions for freedom and democracy' in order to fulfill the prophecy. In any event, Ethiopia, Libya, and Egypt are listed in Scripture as countries conquered by the victorious king of the north because they are allied with Iran, the king of the south (Daniel 11:40-45). Edom, Moab, and Ammon – that is, Turkey and Jordan – will be spared by Assur-Germany because these countries will not be on the side of Iran; they will fully support the king of the north. They will be the closest allies of Assur-Germany in its crafty council against Israel as Psalm 83 portends.

CHAPTER XXI

IDENTIFYING THE NATIONS IN THE WARS OF THE KINGS OF THE NORTH AND SOUTH: "THE GLORIOUS LAND"

Now we can return to Daniel 11:36-45 and state with clarity who is who in this prophecy. The unnamed king of the south of Chapter 11:40 is the Islamic Republic of Iran. The countries of verse 40, which the king of the north enters, defeats and overflows in the Middle East region are Iran, Iraq, and Syria. Together with the captured countries of North Africa – Egypt, Libya, and Ethiopia – they represent a short-lived Muslim-Arab Confederation ruled by the king of the south. "The glorious land" means Israel.

The main hero of the dramatic events of the Daniel prophecy is the king of the north, which is the EU under the leadership of Assur-Germany (verses 36-45). "Tidings out of the East and of the North shall trouble him" (verse 44) refers to the alliance of Russia and China, as these world superpowers fulfill their destinies in the prophesied war of Gog and Magog of Ezekiel 38 and 39. But this war is of the distant future and will take place only after the two preceding wars of Daniel 11:40-45 and Psalm 83. The war scenario described by the Prophet Daniel is not that complicated. The "push" of the king of the south against the king of the north may materialize in Iran's preparation for a nuclear attack against the EU, in its cutting off the oil/gas supply in order to choke the European economy into submission, or in a massive terrorist attack like 9/11 in New York City, or any other significant action that undermine European security. No matter what form the "push" takes, the king of the north will take it seriously and retaliate swiftly with all his might against Iran and its allies in a "blitzkrieg" manner, resulting in the defeat and subjugation of the countries involved. Does it include Israel? It does not seem that it does. Daniel did not say that Israel was defeated and overwhelmed by the king of the north. All he said was that as a result of the "push," the king of the south and his allies were defeated and, in addition, the king of the north entered the Land of Israel. It could be a totally different scenario for the EU entering into the "glorious land." Everybody knows how hard Germany and the EU have tried to push aside the USA from its position as important broker in the ongoing Peace Process and assume this role for themselves.

The Middle East Peace Process has been a priority for the European Union since 1973 and its solution remains one of Europe's primary foreign policy goals. It has pumped tons of money through various channels to the Palestinians as humanitarian and economic development aid, and fully supports the Palestinian demand for a two-state solution. The Arab countries see that America's role in world politics and particularly in the Middle East Peace negotiations has diminished and that the country has failed to live up to its reputation as an honest broker. They are increasingly looking towards rich and dependable Europe, which has already proved its devotion to the Palestinian cause and does not support Israel as strongly as the USA. From another perspective, several years of a protracted and futile Peace Process under the leadership of America has weakened the Israelis politically, morally and even militarily. The Bible compares this Peace Process to Israel's incurable wound. Israelites do not realize that this wound is spiritual—apostasy from God. To fix their problems with the Palestinians, they look to men, even to their enemies, instead of repenting and turning to their God. Despite their "special relations" with Germany, which during WWII killed six million Jews in the Nazi Holocaust, modern Israelis hope that Germany's European Union will be a better protector of Israel than the USA and are inclined to replace their roles in negotiations. It may be that the USA will soon be forced out of the Peace Process as the most influential player and this post will be assumed by the European Union, which is mainly represented by Assur-Germany. It sounds paradoxical, but the fact is that the Israelis and Palestinians both want the EU (Germany) to be a new mediator in the endless peace negotiations. Judah still follows her "lover," even after the murder of six million Jews. Germany has again become one of the most anti-Semitic countries in Europe. It would seem that Judah and Ephraim have forgotten their history. It was the Assyria who destroyed Israel and sent the Ten Tribes into exile.

Indeed, there is nothing new under the sun. The same situation happened in the past: "At that time did king Ahaz of Judea send unto the kings of Assyria to help him and Tilgath-Pilneser king of Assyria came unto him and distressed him, but strengthened him not" (II Chronicles 28:19-20). King Ahaz gave to the Assyrians much gold and silver from the House of the Lord, but the Assyrian king did not assist him. The historical trend has continued. Judah still follows her "lover"—Assur-Germany. In the counterfeit role of peace-maker, Germany will take over leadership of the Peace Process with disastrous consequences. Germany is using Israel, as the major European ally in the region, as a guarantor of stability in the Middle East and counterbalance to the growing influence and aggression of Iran. As soon as the king of the south with its allies is defeated, the king of the north will enter the glorious land, pretending to be the honest peace broker between the Israelis and Palestinian Arabs. The Prophet Hosea informs us that Judah and Ephraim will go for help to Assyria, which is Germany today, but it will not "heal you, nor cure you of your wound." No matter how many bandages are applied to heal Judah's wound — be it the "help" of America or their old "lover" Assur-Germany, be it the Peace Process or Land for

Peace — nothing will help, just as nothing helped in ancient times. This is the most verisimilar version of how the king of the north-Germany "shall enter also into the glorious land" (Daniel 11:40).

But another question has still not been answered: *why* does the king of the north enter into the glorious land? The short and simple answer is—Jerusalem. It is a long-cherished dream of the Vatican to possess and control this ancient holy City. The Vatican is the soul of the king of the north's Empire, its impelling drive, and the power and motivation cementing Roman Catholicism. Possession of Jerusalem is the clearest statement to the world of the veracity of the Roman Catholic religion, the authenticity of its Messiah, and the priority of Christianity above all three monotheistic belief systems. "This is the only way to solve the Middle East conflict," declares one Vatican official. That is why throughout history they fought bloody Crusades against the Muslim-Arab world: to liberate Jerusalem and keep the holy royal city for themselves. The Vatican, which claims that its Christian religious roots lie in the inerrant Hebrew Bible, has ignored the will of God that the Holy Land and Jerusalem belong to the Jews, and is actively involved in all kinds of political games in the attempt to realize its dream. It has clearly taken a biased position against Israel. Why would the Vatican support the Palestinians, reject the Bible, and insist on the creation of a new politically independent Arab State in the land of Israel? Does it really want to end the Israeli-Palestinian conflict and establish a justifiable and comprehensive peace in the region? No—and its claims to the contrary are a facade. Its real intention is for a Germany-led EU Empire to control the Middle East and secure its hydrocarbon resources, and for the Vatican to capture and control Jerusalem, which is the cradle of early Christianity. Its position is not based on God's Bible. It is obviously neither kosher and nor holy. It has forgotten one thing: whoever goes against Israel goes against God, as history and the Scriptures have proven many times. In the near future it will be given a powerful lesson in God Almighty's judgment! The important thing is that the famous Peace Process in the Middle East is not God's plan for the future world. Otherwise, why would Bible tell us that soon all the nations of the world will war against Jerusalem and the modern state of Israel (Psalm 83; Zechariah 12 and 14; Ezekiel 38 and 39)?

In the wars of Daniel 11, the EU will fight against a group of nations led by Iran, the population of which predominately consists of the Shiite branch of Islam. The majority of the Muslim-Arab countries, such as Saudi Arabia, the United Emirates, Jordan, Kuwait, Qatar and others, are of the Sunni branch of Islam, with which the EU has maintained a good relationship. These countries of Sunni descent are scared to death of the prospect of their foe, Shiite Iran, becoming a nuclear power in the region. In its fear of imminent aggression from a nuclear Iran, Saudi Arabia and company may join a long-hated Israel and the West in mutual defense against

Iran. That is why the king of the north will not attack these nations.

Daniel specifically points out that the nations of Edom, Moab, and most of the children of Ammon (which some interpret as the "King and ruling elite") "shall escape out of his hand" (11:41). Moab and Ammon are known as the modern Hashemite Kingdom of Jordan, the population of which is 95% Sunni Islam. Jordan has followed a moderate pro-Western foreign policy and maintained a close relationship with the USA, the EU, and especially Germany. It is the one of only two Arab nations, together with Egypt, that has signed Peace Treaties with Israel. Jordan and Germany have had close relations since 1962. They share many agreements in the political, economic, and cultural spheres. Germany provides technical and financial assistance to the Kingdom, as well as research and development in the areas of environment, renewable energy, agriculture, and education. Jordan has officially enjoyed advanced status with the European Union since December 2010, and is a member of the Euro-Mediterranean free trade area.

It is interesting to note that this friendly relationship between Germany and Jordan originated in ancient times. In the time of King David the Assyrian and Babylonian kings of Mesopotamia decided to challenge the Israelite Kingdom for supremacy in the region. To start the war, they conspired with their proxy Ammonites to provoke David to attack them so that the Assyrians with their allies would join the battle and take care of the Israelites. The Ammonites did as they were told: they assaulted David's messengers of good will and provoked the war. However, the Assyrian plan did not come through—David was victorious in defeating the armies of the Ammonites, Syrians, and Assyrians of Mesopotamia (I Chronicles 19). The same trend will shape the wars between the kings of the north and south of Daniel 11:41: the king of the north, Assur, will remember his friends Moab and Ammon, or Jordan that they "shall escape out of his hands." Jordan will help the king of the north tremendously in his war campaign by providing the use of its territory and fully accommodating all other needs of the EU army.

But what is the most astonishing is that (as they did 3,000 years ago) Assur-Germany will use them again in our time to provoke modern Israelis to attack the children of Lot (i.e. Jordan), and the king of the north (i.e. Germany) with its allies-conspirators will come to assist. We do not know the exact nature of this provocation from the sons of Lot, but the scenario is described by the Prophet Asaph: "Assur also is joined with them to help the children of Lot." The same Ammonite and Moabite nations had a long history of hatred and warfare against Israel. It is they who caused problems for the Jews returning from Babylonian captivity in the time of Ezra and Nehemiah to rebuild Jerusalem and the Temple.

A proper understanding of the prophecy of the preceding wars of the kings of the north and south would help to unlock the mysteries of Psalm 83's wars and its participants. In Daniel

11:45 we learn that Assur, the king of the north, will fall by the hand of God. It will happen "in the glorious land," which is the land of Israel. Nobody will help Assur-Germany during his terrible downfall. This scripture further undermines the theories of some scholars that the beastly power of an Assur-Germany-led EU will be destroyed by the Russians and Chinese: "Assyria will fall by no human sword; a sword, not of mortals, will devour them" (Isaiah 31:8). As can be seen from Psalm 83 and other corroborating prophecies of the Bible, all the nations will also face the judgment of God for their hatred of and rebellion against the Almighty and His people Israel.

CHAPTER XXII

THE CRAFTY COUNCIL OF PSALM 83

As soon as the king of the north (Germany-led Europe) defeats the king of the south (Iran) and its allies, the prophecies of Psalm 83 will begin to unravel. The war with Iran and its allies will not improve the situation in the Middle East. The Arab-Islamic nations will be in turmoil. They will want to annihilate the Jews and their State and take over Jerusalem and the land of Israel. Knowing that the European superpower would support them, they will secretly conspire to convert their ideas into reality and finish with Israel that its name may be remembered no more. To begin the war with Israel openly will be risky because the world community may condemn them as an aggressor and try to stop them. The solution will come from the king of the north who will advise the plotters to use the children of Lot (Jordan) to provoke the Israelis to war.

For Moab and Ammon the provocation business is a familiar trade. They have engaged in it since ancient times when the Assyrian and Babylonian powers wanted to reign supreme in the region and decided to challenge the Israelite United Kingdom to armed battle. They ordered their proxy, the Ammonites, to provoke Israel by attacking it, and then the Mesopotamian kings moved its armies to the Ammonite's defense and destroyed King David's army. The Ammonites did exactly as ordered: they provoked Israel to war, but it resulted in the complete defeat of the Ammonites, Syrians and Assyrian kings (I Chronicles 19). Jordan did it again in the recent past, in November 1966, when it allowed the terrorists from the PLO to conduct guerilla activities against Israel from the territory controlled by Jordan. It is called "Samu provocation." Three Israelite soldiers were killed in a mine attack. The Israeli Defense Force attacked the village of as-Samu in the Jordanian-occupied West Bank, captured or killed the terrorists and destroyed Jordanian armed units that engaged the Israelis. That was the "casus belli" of the 1967 Six-Day War.

The other provocation happened a couple of years earlier, in 1964, when the Hashemite Kingdom began construction of the Headwater Diversion Plan that would divert the waters of the Banias Stream before they entered Israel and the Sea of Galilee. The IDF attacked the diversion works and prevented their completion. These kinds of provocations perpetuate a prolonged chain of border violence that link directly to the events leading to war. Yet the strongest and the most effective way to provoke Israel to war is to close off Jewish access to the holiest site on the Temple Mount in

Jerusalem, where the Solomon Temple once stood. Jordan has authority over the Dome of the Rock and its Ministry of *Awqaf* in Amman is responsible for its operation, security and maintenance. The Israeli police help Muslim religious authorities to enforce order. It can also blow up the Dome or Al-Aqsa Mosque, pretending that the Jews are to blame, and fabricate evidence—this would immediately rouse the indignation of the Arab-Muslim world against the Israelis, making war absolutely inevitable.

The Jews watch as America loses its weight and authority among the world powers and becomes preoccupied with many other global problems and ethnic conflicts; their leaders are too weak and will-broken to defend Israel. Instead, they choose the Palestinian side, ignoring the safety and security of Israel; in doing so, the USA seeks to boost its image in the Arab-Muslim world and secure the flow of oil into America. Recently, the Israelites completed the building of a 142 mile-long and 15 feet-high defensive wall along its southern border. This barrier is equipped with military cameras, radars, and other electronic surveillance equipment. Israel plans to construct a similar wall in the northern region of the Golan Heights on the border with Syria. Although Israel has done everything it can to protect itself from its enemies, as the terrorist activity intensifies and the possibility of imminent war increases, the Israelis will ask Germany to "enter into the glorious land" and help to defend it from the aggressive surrounding nations. Instead of repenting and seeking the protection of God, the Israelites foolishly put their trust in the Germans.

The Israelis will allow Germany to enter "the glorious land" as international peacekeepers. The Germans may act under the UN umbrella and use military force to stabilize the region. This strategy of utilizing the UN and acting under its umbrella to pursue its own imperial agenda is well known to Germany and proved effective in 1999 when it orchestrated the break-up of the former Yugoslavia and took control of the small countries of the Balkan Peninsula and the Mediterranean Sea. To help its peacekeeping mission, Germany will invite its old friend and reliable ally Turkey. Edom-Turkey, as the closest ally of Germany, could enter Israel as one of the ten kings prophesied in Daniel 7:24. Although Turkey is not a member state of the European Union today, there are indications that it will be in the near future. The prophet Asaph foresaw the significance of Edom in the crafty council of plotting nations, and named him first among those nations. Assur-Germany will be the leading force of this confederation against Israel; it will call the shots in determining the nature of this military campaign. As in the past, when Assyrians destroyed Jerusalem and Israel and the Edomites helped them, so it will be again, when Assur-Germany-led EU armed forces enter the "glorious land "— Edom-Turkey will be "as one of them" according to the words of Prophet Obadiah (1:11). It is certain that countries such as Iran, Syria, Iraq, and Egypt, as a result of Daniel's wars of the kings of the north and south, will not be able take any action in the following wars of Psalm 83, as they will be defeated and subjugated by the victorious king of the north.

Daniel did not disclose many, if any, details concerning the way that the king of the north will conduct his military campaign after "enter[ing] the glorious land" of Israel. What are his actions after that? There is one small detail that may help: "but tiding out of the east and out of the north shall trouble him" (Daniel 11:44). If in the past the ships of Chittim (11:30), who represented the Roman Empire, prevented King Antiochus IV from capturing Egypt, in the future it will be the powers of Gog and Magog that will stop Daniel's king of the north from capturing the Middle East, Africa and the rest of the world. The northern powers mainly represent Russia; and the eastern powers represent ancient Chittim, who moved out of southern Europe (Italy) to Central Asia and founded the country called China. Dr. Ernest Martin explains this historical process in his writings.

On the other hand, the eastern forces of China may well be represented by the multitudinous Hebrew descendants of Joktan (Genesis 10:26-30), as thoroughly explained by Phelps and Kwok. It will be the powers of Russia and China with their Islamic allies, as stated in Ezekiel 38:3-6, that will challenge and halt the beastly European power on its way to world domination. The ancient non-Israelite prophet Balaam (Numbers 24:24) predicted that, "Ships shall come from the coast of Chittim, and shall afflict Asshur, and shall afflict Eber, and he also shall perish forever." In another translation, "he also shall perish" appears as "but they too will come to ruin," or "but they, too, will be utterly destroyed." Interestingly enough, this prophecy has a strong connection to Assur, the king of the north or EU, with Daniel 11:44 and Ezekiel 38 and 39 speaking of the terrible downfall of Assur and the hordes of Gog at the hand of God Almighty.

Some people may wonder why, if Iran, Libya and Ethiopia will be defeated and conquered by the king of the north in the wars of Daniel 11:40-43, their names are mentioned as participants (i.e. allies) in the war of Gog and Magog? Well, the explanation is not complicated. Although those countries will be defeated and captured by the German-led coalition of the EU, its people will not be annihilated, and after the demise of the king of the north's Empire, Iran, Libya and Ethiopia will slowly regain their independence and restore their nations to their previous status. Besides, there is considerable time for such transformation between the end of the wars of Psalm 83 and the beginning of the Gog and Magog wars of Ezekiel 38 and 39.

The intervention of the northern and eastern powers will infuriate the king of the north, and in his madness "he shall go forth with great fury to destroy, and utterly to make away many" (Daniel 11:44). It is not clear here if the Israelites will be among those numerous victims of Assur; they likely will because the Prophet Isaiah says: "O My people who dwell in Zion, do not fear the Assyrian who strikes you with the rod and lifts up his staff against you, the way Egypt did. For in a very little while My indignation against you will be spent and My anger will be directed to their destruction" (Isaiah 10:24-25). It is God who gave the king of the north-Assur the power to capture the Middle East, including Israel, and African countries, for solely correctional purposes: "O Assur, the rod of Mine anger." Because of Assur's arrogance and unnecessary cruelty, God will not let Assyria go unpunished: "Yet he means not so, neither does his heart think so; but it is in his heart to destroy and cut off nations, not a few" (10:7). God swore an oath: "Surely, as I have planned, so it will be, and as I have purposed, so it will happen. I will break the Assyrian in My land and upon My mountains tread him under foot: then shall his yoke depart from off them, and his burden depart from off their shoulders" (14:24-25). These prophecies of Isaiah are heavily connected to the prophecies of Daniel, as both speak of the same Assur as the king of the north in the End time. Isaiah confirms that Assur will invade Israel and, as Daniel describes, face defeat in the Land of Israel, or "come to his end, and there is nobody who could help him" (Daniel 11:40-45). This prophecy has not yet been fulfilled because the wars of the kings of the north and south have not yet started and Assyria has not been defeated in the land of Israel.

The Prophet Daniel did not elaborate on the actions of the Germany-led European coalition after its troops entered "the glorious land." After the series of peace negotiations, which will result at in a deadlock, the Israelis will realize that the king of the north is not their friend and not interested in defending it and bringing about peace and security with its Arab neighbors, but rather in pursuing its own political agenda. When the Germans see that the Israelis have figured out their real intentions, they will quit playing political games, pretending to treat the Israelites as a friend and to be a peacemaker, and mobilize the rest of its allies from Arab-Muslim countries to declare war against Israel and seize Jerusalem, thus initiating the prophecy of Psalm 83. This scenario is also the subject of Zechariah's prophecies: "Behold, I will make Jerusalem a cup of trembling unto all the people round about" (Zechariah 12:2). As a result of this battle, the Israelis will "devour all the people round about, on the right hand and on the left: and Jerusalem shall be inhabited again in her own place, even in Jerusalem" (Zech. 12:6). It will be an impossible task to defeat Israel because the Almighty will defend it and will be its fortress, as it written: "Fear you not; for I am with you: be not dismayed; for I am your God: I will strengthen you; yes, I will help you; yes, I will uphold you with the right hand of my righteousness" (Isaiah 41:10). Having such assurances from the Almighty, how could Richardson doubt and distrust Israel's ability to overcome all of its enemies and become victorious? Israel will put its trust in God, and then nothing will harm it: "No weapon that is fashioned against you shall succeed, and you shall confute every tongue that rises against you in judgment. This is the heritage of the servants of the Lord and their vindication from Me, declares the Lord" (Isaiah 54:17).

God warns nations that He will make Jerusalem a burdensome stone; whoever tries to lift it will be "cut in pieces." Yet the prophet says that "the city shall be taken, and the houses rifled, and the women ravished. Half of the city will go into exile, but the rest of the people will not be taken from the city" (Zechariah 14:2). It seems that Jerusalem is to be captured by international German-led armies and enter one last bloodbath before God returns. At this point, the surrounding Israel aggressive Arab nations will be destroyed by IDF, and the main power of the Arab-Muslim world — Iran with its allies — had already been subjugated by the king of the north, which is Assur-Germany with its European allies. The Vatican, Germany, and EU will double-cross the Israelis of their peacekeeping intentions and will capture the City for themselves. Some commentators think that this battle for Jerusalem will trigger events that lead to a nuclear World War III. At this moment God will intervene on the side of the Israelites and seek to destroy them that come against Jerusalem. That is how the king of the north and his multitude of allies will be destroyed in the land of Israel, and no one will help him to withstand God's judgment. Amazingly, even Solomon's Song of Songs sheds some light on the fate of Assur-Germany's coalition: "I charge you, O daughters of Jerusalem, by the roes, and by the hinds of the field, that you stir not up, nor awake my love, till it pleases"

(Songs 2:7). The famous Jewish commentators of the Bible – Rashi, Sforno and Metzudat David – translated the "daughters of Jerusalem" as the heathen nations destined to descend on Jerusalem. According to these scholars, it will be the king of the north's coalition of the EU and the Middle Eastern Arab-Muslim nations that will surround Jerusalem in latter days. In allegorical language, the Song of Songs warns those nations not to go against God and His people Israel, or God will remove the divine protection of their souls, and they will become as the defenseless field animals subjected to slaughter. Here is the proper translation of the verse above: "I adjure you, O nations who are destined to descend on Jerusalem, lest you become as defenseless as gazelles or hinds of the field, if you dare cause hatred or disturb the love while it yet gratifies, that is, if you disobey God and go to war against Jerusalem." God chooses holy Jerusalem as His desired place of dwelling: "Blessed be the Lord out of Zion, who lives at Jerusalem" (Psalm 135:21). He wants all people of the world to worship Him there. Jerusalem is the true significant spiritual center not only for His people Israel but for all nations of the earth. They will call Jerusalem 'the throne of the Lord.' "Pray for the peace of Jerusalem: they shall prosper that love you" (Psalm 122:6).

After enjoying glorious victories, world-wide fame and heroic achievement, Assur-Germany will endure utter defeat, severe punishment, tribulations, and calamities. Many German people will be killed as a result of God's judgment. The Prophet Zechariah stated that, "The pride of Assyria shall be brought down" (10:11). The entire book of the Prophet Nahum is devoted to the final punishment of Assur-Germany, whose history has been continually filled with cruel atrocities and wickedness. As the prophet says, all the nations on earth have been its victims: "Your shepherds are sleeping, O king of Assyria. There is no healing of your bruise; your wound is grievous: all that hear the report of you shall clap their hands over you: for upon whom has not your wickedness passed continually" (Nahum 3:18-19)? As the Prophet Isaiah describes, God has vowed to "break the Assyrian in My land and upon My mountains tread him under foot" (14:25). These future prophecies of the fate of Assur-Germany should prove instructive to those theologians who erroneously maintain that the Assyrians of Psalm 83 are Syrians, Iraqis or Turks. In describing the future prophetic wars of Psalm 83 and Ezekiel 38 and 39, those scholars find no place in their theologies for Germany and the European Union, contrary to the opinion of Bible's prophets. Their interpretation of the nations involved in the crafty council could not be further from the Biblical truth.

To clarify again the order of the prophetic events according to the Bible verses, the wars between the kings of the north and south of the Book of Daniel ought to precede the wars of Psalm 83. Only by understanding the prophecies of Daniel (11:36-45) can one discern the participant-nations conspiring against Israel in Psalm 83. There is plenty of Scriptural prophesies of resurrection in our days of the Holy Roman Empire under the undisputed political leadership of Germany and the Catholic Vatican. In the famous and extremely prophetic dream of Nebuchadnezzar, Daniel envisioned the fourth kingdom to be as strong as iron (the Roman Empire), with two feet that were part iron and part clay, indicating that this kingdom will be divided and will be partly strong and partly broken. The political and economic situation of the eastern and western parts of the European Union today perfectly fits Daniel's description of this empire of the End time. For example, the ten toes indicate the final ten nations of the EU, a body of iron and clay that will be led by Assur-Germany in the war against the king of the south, which is Iran (Daniel 2:40-43; 7:23-24; 11:40-43).

Historians and scholars of the Bible have made many incorrect assumptions and contradictory decisions in attempting to identify the plotters of the confederacy in Psalm 83. If they were familiar with the outcome of the wars of the king of the north and the king of the south, they would realize that neither Iran, Iraq, and Syria, nor Egypt, Lybia, and Ethiopia, could possibly take part in a bloody crusade against Israel because all of these countries were defeated and subjugated by the victorious king of the north, that is, Assur-Germany. Also it would be clear for them why the king of the north will spare Edom (Turkey) and Ammon and Moab (modern Jordan, the children of Lot in Psalm 83). These countries will escape the wrath of the king of the north not by accident—Turkey and Jordan are the closest allies of Assur-Germany not only against the armies of the king of the south, but also against Israel in Psalm 83. It will be the children of Lot (Jordan) who will provoke the war and, as the prophecy says, the German-led coalition of the EU and the rest of the surrounding Israel Arab-Muslim plotters that will come to its aid. We have written about these matters at length in previous chapters.

Not all German people will perish. Whoever survives will repent of their evil ways and serve God. The Almighty understands that this oldest civilization has also made valuable contributions to the world in science, music, literature, art, architecture, and philosophy—the Germans have literally shaped this world's way of thinking over the centuries. The remarkably hard working, honest and highly intelligent people of Germany will be forgiven and even blessed by God together with the people of Egypt and Israel: "In that day shall there be a highway out of Egypt to Assyria, and the Assyrian shall come into Egypt, and the Egyptian into Assyria, and the Egyptians shall serve with the Assyrians (Isaiah 19:23). This "highway" is understood not as a literal highway of Isaiah (11:16) to facilitate the return of the Israelites to their home land after Egyptian bondage, but as a spiritual union between Assyria, Egypt, and Israel. It signifies the ideal of peace, faith in the God of Israel, and mutual cooperation. Assyria, Egypt, and Israel will finally find their way to God. They must experience refinement through God's correctional judgments, and then they will repent of their evil deeds and begin service to their Creator. "Blessed be Egypt My people, and Assyria the work of My hands, and Israel Mine inheritance," says the Lord (Isaiah 19:25). These prophecies are additional evidence, contrary to the opinions of some theologians, that the Assyrian people have not disappeared, that they are around, alive and well, recognized under another name – Germany – and significant to the geopolitical eschatology of the End times.